FORTY VARIATIONS
ON A THEME BY BEETHOVEN

SONATA IN F MINOR
FOR VIOLIN AND PIANO

RECENT RESEARCHES IN THE MUSIC OF THE NINETEENTH AND EARLY TWENTIETH CENTURIES

Rufus Hallmark and D. Kern Holoman, general editors

A-R Editions, Inc., publishes seven series of musicological editions
that present music brought to light in the course of current research:

Recent Researches in the Music of the Middle Ages and Early Renaissance
Charles Atkinson, general editor

Recent Researches in the Music of the Renaissance
James Haar, general editor

Recent Researches in the Music of the Baroque Era
Christoph Wolff, general editor

Recent Researches in the Music of the Classical Era
Eugene K. Wolf, general editor

Recent Researches in the Music of the Nineteenth and Early Twentieth Centuries
Rufus Hallmark and D. Kern Holoman, general editors

Recent Researches in American Music
H. Wiley Hitchcock, general editor

Recent Researches in the Oral Traditions of Music
Philip V. Bohlman, general editor

Each *Recent Researches* edition is devoted to works
by a single composer or to a single genre of composition.
The contents are chosen for their potential interest to scholars
and performers, then prepared for publication according to the
standards that govern the making of all reliable historical editions.

Subscribers to any of these series, as well as patrons of subscribing institutions,
are invited to apply for information about the "Copyright-Sharing Policy"
of A-R Editions, Inc., under which policy any part of an edition
may be reproduced free of charge for study or performance.

For information contact

A-R EDITIONS, INC.
801 Deming Way
Madison, Wisconsin 53717

(608) 836-9000

RECENT RESEARCHES IN THE MUSIC OF THE NINETEENTH
AND EARLY TWENTIETH CENTURIES • VOLUME 21

Archduke Rudolph of Austria

FORTY VARIATIONS ON A THEME BY BEETHOVEN
for Piano

SONATA IN F MINOR FOR VIOLIN AND PIANO

Edited by Susan Kagan

A-R Editions, Inc.
Madison

A violin part, edited by Josef Suk, is available from the publisher.

A recording of the violin sonata has been issued by Koch International (KIC 7082), performed by Josef Suk (violin) and Susan Kagan (piano).

© 1992 by A-R Editions, Inc.
All rights reserved
Printed in the United States of America

Rudolph, Archduke of Austria, 1788–1831.
   [Aufgabe von Ludwig van Beethoven gedichtet, vierzig Mahl verändert]
   Forty variations on a theme by Beethoven : for piano ; Sonata in F minor for violin and piano / Archduke Rudolph of Austria ; edited by Susan Kagan.
   p. of music. — (Recent researches in the music of the nineteenth and early twentieth centuries, ISSN 0193-5364 ; v. 21)
   The theme of the variations is Beethoven's O Hoffnung, WoO 200.
   Includes Beethoven's emendations to the variations and an earlier version of the sonata.
   ISBN 0-89579-275-3
   1. Variations (Piano)   2. Sonatas (Violin and piano)—Scores.
I. Kagan, Susan. II. Beethoven, Ludwig van, 1770–1827. O Hoffnung.
III. Rudolph, Archduke of Austria, 1788–1831. Sonatas, violin, piano, F minor. 1992. IV. Title. V. Title: 40 variations on a theme by Beethoven. VI. Title: Variations on a theme by Beethoven.
VII. Series.
M2.R23834 vol. 21
[M3.1]
                                                              92-761694
                                                                  CIP
                                                                     M

Contents

PREFACE
   The Composer   vii
   The Music   viii
   The Sources   x
   Editorial Methods   xi
   Critical Notes   xii
   Notes   xiii

PLATE   xv

FORTY VARIATIONS ON A THEME BY BEETHOVEN   1
   for Piano

SONATA IN F MINOR FOR VIOLIN AND PIANO   39
   Allegro   41
   Adagio   62
   Menuetto: Allegro molto   69
   Allegro assai quasi presto   82

APPENDIX 1
   Beethoven's Emendations to the *Forty Variations*:
   Facsimile and Transcription of CS-KRa A 4375   103

APPENDIX 2
   Sonata in F Minor for Violin and Piano, Earlier Version:
   Facsimiles of CS-KRa A 4405, A 4407   115
     Allegro   117
     Scherzo. Allegro   124
     Finale. Allegro assai   125
     Adagio con esspressione   132
     [Adagio] draft   135

Preface

This edition presents two compositions representative of the works of Archduke Rudolph of Austria (1788–1831), who had the unique privilege of studying and composing under the aegis of the most famous composer of his time, Ludwig van Beethoven. For most music historians and music lovers, Archduke Rudolph is known principally for his role as Beethoven's patron and as the dedicatee of such famous and important works as the *Archduke* Trio, op. 97, and the *Missa Solemnis*, op. 123. Less known is the fact that the Archduke Rudolph—a Habsburg prince by birth and a priest of the Roman Catholic church (later a cardinal-archbishop) by vocation—was a serious composer who, in his studies with Beethoven for more than two decades, produced a small but well-crafted body of works, three of which were published during his lifetime. The music published in this edition includes one of those works published earlier, the *Forty Variations on a Theme by Beethoven*, as well as a sonata for violin and piano that has remained in manuscript.

The Composer

Archduke Rudolph, the youngest of the sixteen children born to Leopold, grand duke of Tuscany, and his wife, Princess Maria Ludovica of Spain, was brought up in Vienna under the supervision of his eldest brother, Franz, who became emperor of Austria in 1792.[1] All the imperial children received a wide-ranging and thorough education to prepare them for the positions—military, governmental, or religious—they would eventually hold in the ruling monarchy. The Habsburg line included several composers and music patrons. Emperor Franz's own interest in music ensured its place among the cultural subjects in the children's curriculum. The court composer, Anton Teyber, was entrusted with their music education.

Rudolph, like his brothers, was at first prepared for a military career, but because of his delicate health (he inherited the Habsburg predisposition to epilepsy and was subject to seizures throughout his life), he turned to a religious vocation and in 1805 took the minor vows of the Catholic church. That same year he was appointed coadjutor to the archbishop of Olmütz (now Olomouc, Czechoslovakia) with rights of succession, becoming archbishop himself in 1819 and cardinal-archbishop in 1820. During his tenure as archbishop his principal residence was the archbishop's palace in Kremsier (now Kroměříž, Czechoslovakia), although he spent large amounts of time in the Imperial Palace, the Hofburg, in Vienna and in various health spas such as those in Baden bei Wien, Teplitz, and Bad Ischl, where he underwent periodic cures for his various ailments. It was in Baden that Archduke Rudolph suffered the cerebral hemorrhage that ended his life at the age of forty-three.

Rudolph's association with Beethoven began, to the best of our knowledge, during the winter of 1803–4, when the archduke had achieved a certain amount of independence by being given his own apartments and retinue of servants in the Hofburg. An accomplished pianist, the fifteen-year-old Rudolph performed in the drawing rooms of the music-loving Viennese aristocracy, where Beethoven was also a frequent visitor. Although precise records are lacking, evidence points to the years 1803–4 as the time when Rudolph became Beethoven's student, first in piano and, shortly thereafter, in composition also.[2]

In 1808 Beethoven dedicated the Fourth Piano Concerto, op. 58, to the archduke—the first of over a dozen dedications that included many of Beethoven's most valued works—and in 1809 Rudolph joined with the Princes Kinsky and Lobkowitz in arranging a lifetime annuity for Beethoven that would ensure his remaining in Vienna. For the archduke, keeping Beethoven in Vienna was not only an act of patriotism; it also guaranteed the continuation of his composition lessons with the composer.

The earliest documentation of Rudolph's lessons with Beethoven dates from the years 1809–10, when Beethoven, during the siege of Vienna by the French army, occupied himself with putting together extracts from various theoretical works for his pupil's instruction. While in exile with the other members of the emperor's family in Hungary during the winter months, Rudolph composed two of his earliest compositions, dated March and May 1810.[3] By the end of 1810, after the return of the imperial family to Vienna, a teaching relationship was clearly in progress, as attested by a letter from Beethoven to Rudolph in December of that year apologizing for missing a scheduled lesson—the first of dozens of similar letters sent over the next fourteen years. Not surprisingly, the bulk of Archduke Rudolph's compositions dates from the period 1810–24, coinciding with the time he actively studied with Beethoven.

Despite a time-consuming schedule fulfilling the duties and obligations connected with the archbishopric as well as his place in the monarchy, Rudolph devoted seemingly most of his spare time to music—to playing, composing, and collecting and cataloging his vast music library. Far from being a dilettante, Archduke Rudolph worked hard and seriously at composing. This is documented not only by his collected oeuvre (described below) but by the hundreds of pages of sketches in which, much like Beethoven, he worked and reworked his ideas. Beethoven's involvement in Rudolph's music can be seen in the many corrections and suggested changes he indicated on several of the archduke's manuscripts. For the most part, Beethoven deals with small details affecting melodic shape, rhythmic articulation, or chord voicing; but in some compositions, such as the *Forty Variations,* his emendations include the rewriting of passages of several measures. It is noteworthy, however, that, by and large, Beethoven perceived his pedagogical role as one in which he refrained from imposing his own powerful personality on his student and allowed Rudolph to express his own voice as a composer.

After 1824 Archduke Rudolph appears to have stopped composing, perhaps because much of his inspiration as a composer was tied to the teaching of Beethoven, and at this time Beethoven became increasingly isolated from the world around him. Following Beethoven's death Rudolph involved himself in other endeavors;[4] he became preoccupied with his last will and testament, writing several versions of it. For the music world the most important paragraph in that will was the one in which he bequeathed his music collection to the library of the Gesellschaft der Musikfreunde in Vienna. When this institution had been established in 1814 and royal sponsorship sought, it was Archduke Rudolph, the musical representative of the imperial family, who became its first Protector. Three years after his death, in 1834, the vast collection of music manuscripts (including important Beethoven autographs), printed music, and books on music, which had been amassed by the archduke since his childhood and carefully cataloged in his hand and maintained in the palace library in Kremsier, was shipped to Vienna, where it became the core of one of the great music libraries in the world today.[5]

Following stipulations in his will, Archduke Rudolph's heart was removed from his body after his death and placed within the walls of the Cathedral of St. Wenceslas in Olmütz, the seat of his archbishopric. A small bust of Rudolph placed in a niche on one wall commemorates this spot today. His body lies in the Habsburg family crypt in Vienna.

The Music

The bulk of Archduke Rudolph's compositions are preserved today in two locations. The majority, all autographs, are in the archives of the Státní Zámek (State Castle) in Kroměříž, Czechoslovakia, Rudolph's former residence; about two dozen works (most of them copies, but a few autographs also) are in the archive of the Gesellschaft der Musikfreunde in Vienna.[6] The archduke's total oeuvre, which is fully described and numbered by the author in her thematic catalog (see note 3) can be summarized as follows: twenty-seven completed compositions (Thematic catalog, nos. 1–27); thirty-five unfinished compositions (Thematic catalog, nos. U 1–U 35), of which some lack only one or two pages to be complete; twenty-eight transcriptions, arrangements, or manuscript copies of works by other composers, principally Beethoven, Mozart, and Handel (Thematic catalog, nos. T 1–T 28); and hundreds of pages of miscellaneous sketches, ranging in length from a few measures to drafts of several pages.

The three works published during Archduke Rudolph's lifetime were the *Forty Variations* (S. A. Steiner & Co., Vienna, 1819); Sonata in A Major for Clarinet and Piano (S. A. Steiner & Co., 1822); and a Fugue variation for the set of fifty variations solicited by Anton Diabelli on his own waltz theme and published by him in 1824.[7]

Beethoven's corrections and suggested changes can be found on six of Archduke Rudolph's compositions—five of them Rudolph's autographs and one the work of a copyist. The number, extent, and significance of Beethoven's revisions vary from one work to another, with the greatest amount—and the most wide-ranging—in the *Forty Variations,* the work that, at Beethoven's insistence, first brought Archduke Rudolph before the public.

Archduke Rudolph composed primarily for the piano, either as a solo instrument or in an instrumental or vocal duo. Among the instrumental works those that include woodwinds—especially clarinet, basset horn, and czakan (csákány)—predominate, undoubtedly owing to the presence in Rudolph's household of two accomplished woodwind players, the brothers Counts Ferdinand and Franz de Troyer, who served as his chamberlains. Of the few songs Rudolph attempted, most were left unfinished, and his one orchestral work, a set of twelve *Ländler,* was composed originally for piano duet.

The prevalence in his total oeuvre of small forms, particularly variations, suggests that the archduke was less comfortable with large-scale structures. Only two sonatas are extant in his instrumental music, both of them written closer to the beginning of his composing career, ca. 1812.[8] Both are characteristic of the period, using the traditional sonata-allegro and ternary forms. But it was in the variation works that Rudolph excelled, where he let his imagination flower in original and often ingenious musical ideas; and nowhere is this better exemplified than in the *Forty Variations.*

In musical syntax Archduke Rudolph also tended to conform to the traditions of his time, rarely venturing much beyond the harmonic vocabulary of the period. His language is substantially diatonic; indeed, a characteristic Beethoven emendation in Rudolph's manuscripts is one that intensifies the dominant function or chromaticizes a bland melodic line. In general, Rudolph limited himself to the genres, forms, and musical language of his period, content to float in the mainstream of compositional styles common to the early nineteenth century.

The Forty Variations

The genesis of the *Forty Variations* (Thematic catalog, no. 9) was a four-measure song, or *Liedthema,* "O Hoffnung, o Hoffnung" (WoO 200), written out by

Beethoven in the spring of 1818 as an assignment for Archduke Rudolph in variations composition. The brief text, "O Hoffnung, o Hoffnung! Du stählst die Herzen, vertreibst die Schmerzen" (O Hope, O Hope! You steel the heart, you soften the pain) is in Beethoven's hand also; since it cannot be traced, it may well be that Beethoven himself is the author.[9] After receiving Beethoven's theme the archduke set to work composing the variations and sent a draft to Beethoven in the fall of 1818. Beethoven wrote suggestions for small changes on five sheets, which are reproduced and transcribed in Appendix 1. Several letters in the Beethoven correspondence[10] give a detailed history of Rudolph's work on the variations: Beethoven was clearly impressed, and in the spring of 1819 he suggested that they be published. Beethoven characterized the variations as "masterly," personified Rudolph as a "favorite of the Muses," as "the spirit of Apollo," and arranged with S. A. Steiner, his own publisher at that time, to bring out the variations. He even suggested a title page: "Theme or exercise set by L. v. Beeth[oven] on which forty variations have been written and dedicated to his teacher by *His Excellency the Composer*." When the variations appeared in print at the end of 1819, the title page (shown in plate 1) read (in translation): "Exercise | composed by Ludwig van Beethoven, | varied forty times | and dedicated to its author | by his student | R. E. H. [*Rudolph Erzherzog*]." Two reviews of the publication, both highly laudatory, appeared in widely read journals in 1820—one in January, the other in June.[11]

In its final, finished version, the *Forty Variations* is a work of large scope, despite the fact that thirty-five of the variations follow the four-measure construction of the theme. The work opens with an eighty-eight measure introduction in G minor, marked "Adagio"; in it the melodic material, treated in fantasy style, anticipates elements of the G-major theme, which follows.[12] In the first four variations Rudolph adopts a procedure similar to that used by Beethoven in his so-called *Eroica* Variations, op. 35, beginning with a single melodic line and adding contrapuntal voices one by one, until at variation 4 all four voices appear in the chorale style of the original theme. With variation 5, marked by a change in tempo and a departure from the chorale setting, Rudolph uses an imaginative and highly resourceful array of musical styles and techniques to produce continual variety within the four-measure format, including imitation, changes in meter, tempo, and dynamics, florid figuration, and various rhythmic devices such as triplets, syncopation, and so one. The last five variations expand in length and complexity and follow a traditional design in including a slow variation (var. 36, in improvisatory style), a march (var. 37), and a minuet (var. 39). Variation 40, the finale, is the longest and most complex, a rondo with two contrasting sections followed by a fugue of some ninety measures. Because of the counterpoint some of the passages in the fugue are rather awkward to play, but, in general, Archduke Rudolph's writing for piano is idiomatic and of moderate difficulty.

Sonata in F Minor for Violin and Piano

The Sonata in F Minor (Thematic catalog, no. 20) is one of two works Archduke Rudolph composed for the violin (the other is a set of variations on a theme by Prince Louis Ferdinand of Prussia). Rudolph's apparent lack of interest in composing for the violin may be attributed to the absence in his household retinue of a violinist with abilities comparable to those of the Troyer brothers. The genesis of this sonata, however, which dates from ca. 1812, may well have been the archduke's contact with the famous French violinist Pierre Rode (1774–1830), who was visiting Vienna at that time. Rudolph joined forces with Rode to give the first performance of Beethoven's Violin Sonata in G Major, op. 96, which is dedicated to Rudolph and which was performed twice within two weeks at Prince Lobkowitz's palace. The opportunity to play with a performer of Rode's stature might have been the inspiration for Archduke Rudolph's own sonata.

The autograph of an early draft of the Sonata in F Minor (reproduced in facsimile in Appendix 2) is in the Kroměříž archive; some pages of the third movement are missing. Four manuscript copies, each in a different hand, are extant—three of them are in the Gesellschaft der Musikfreunde in Vienna, and one is in the Musiksammlung of the Landesbibliothek in Gotha, Germany. Of the four copies, two are of the piano part only (see Sources for full description). The existence of so many copies suggests the sonata had some popularity, at least in Archduke Rudolph's musical circle. The finished work differs greatly from the autograph draft; only the basic thematic ideas for each movement were retained, and the final version was extensively revised and refined.

The violin sonata is in the traditional four-movement structure; the first and last movements, in F minor (Allegro and Allegro assai quasi presto), are in sonata form, framing a slow movement (Adagio) in D-flat major and a Menuetto (with two Trios) in B-flat major. The first movement relies basically on a single thematic idea that is clearly derived from the main theme of the first movement of Mozart's Quartet for Piano and Strings in G Minor, K. 478—a work that Archduke Rudolph had transcribed for two pianos (only the transcription of the string parts in piano score survives among his sketches). The second theme is rhythmically identical with the first but contrasting in tonality, dynamics, and character.

The slow movement is in song form, lyrical in nature, with the middle section in minor. It is worth noting that the tonality of this movement in relationship to the first (the flattened sixth degree of the scale) is one much favored by Schubert and, to a lesser degree, Beethoven. In the reprise the accompaniment is embellished with a triplet figure, and in the coda Rudolph offers a harmonic surprise with a brief excursion into the remote key of A major.

The tonality of the Menuetto is initially confusing: while the key signature indicates B-flat major, the first section not only begins and ends in F major but opens with an F major chord as well; not until the final cadence of the Menuetto is B-flat major firmly established. Each of the Trios is in a contrasting tonality; the first, in B-flat minor, is canonic, and the second, in D major, features dotted rhythms. According to the autograph sketch, Rudolph originally titled the movement "Scherzo," but evidently decided that "Menuetto" was more in keeping with its dance character, which is somewhat restrained.

The finale has two contrasting themes, both of which are characterized by rapid figuration that propels the movement along despite its length. In this movement, as well as in the rest of the sonata, the violin writing allows for a good deal of technical display.

The Sources

Forty Variations

S   Aufgabe | von Ludwig van Beethoven gedichtet, | Vierzig Mahl verändert | *und ihrem* Verfasser *gewidmet* | von | seinem Schuler | R: E: H: | [Opus] I | Wien, bei S. A. Steiner und Comp.
In the lower left quadrant: [Plate] No. 3080
In the lower right quadrant: Preis [blank]

A   Kroměříž, Czechoslovakia, Státní Zámek a Zahrady, Historicko-Umělecké Fondy, Hudební Archív [CS-KRa], MS A 4373

G   Vienna, Gesellschaft der Musikfreunde [A-Wgm], MS Q 15075

Source S, the first edition of the *Forty Variations*, appeared at the end of 1819 as part of the series Musée musical des clavicinistes. The exemplar used for the present edition is at the Gesellschaft der Musikfreunde, Vienna.[13]

The autograph sketches and drafts of the *Forty Variations* preserved in the archive in Kroměříž encompass two versions of the work and six pages of Beethoven's autograph sketches for suggested emendations. Under the library sigla A 4372–75, this group of manuscripts consists of (a) a draft (version I) [A 4372], twenty-six pages; (b) a draft (version II) [A 4373], forty-one pages (= source A); (c) "O Hoffnung" theme, one page, and crossed-out pencil sketches, five pages [A 4374]; (d) Beethoven sketches (emendations, five pages; suggested title, one page) [A 4375]. Version I appears to be a preliminary draft, with few expression marks and lacking some variations added to version II. Both versions were corrected in detail by Beethoven, sometimes directly on Rudolph's work, sometimes in the nearest margin. Version II is clearly a revision of version I, but it too underwent some significant changes, chief among them those indicated by Beethoven in the five pages of corrections referring to the revised version (see App. 1).

Source G, a manuscript copy in the Gesellschaft der Musikfreunde, in a careful and professional hand, incorporates all the corrections made in A (version II) and closely approximates the published edition.

Evaluation of the Sources

The principal source for the present publication of the *Forty Variations* is S, the edition published in Vienna in 1819 by S. A. Steiner and Co. This edition, in an oblong format on thirty-one pages, has a crowded and sometimes confusing appearance owing to the close spacing between systems. As noted, the engraver of the Steiner print attempted to be very faithful to both the copyist's manuscript and version II as emended; however, a careful comparison with the latter two sources indicates that some additional expression marks and details, lacking in the manuscripts, appear in the print. One may conclude, therefore, that the Steiner publication represents a final text. Metronome markings appear only in the printed edition and are of unknown provenance but may have been added by Rudolph at a proof stage.[14]

Because of the cramped format of the principal source, there are many ambiguities in the placement of various expression marks. In most cases, clarification is provided by both A, Rudolph's autograph, and G, the Gesellschaft copy. An explanation of editorial principles concerning corrections and variants can be found in the Editorial Methods.

Sonata in F Minor for Violin and Piano

A   Kroměříž, Czechoslovakia, Státní Zámek a Zahrady, Historicko-Umělecké Fondy, Hudební Archív [CS-KRa], MSS A 4405, A 4407.[15] [Autograph score]

I   Vienna, Gesellschaft der Musikfreunde [A-Wgm], MS Q 17758. [Copyist score and violin part]

II   Gotha, Germany, Forschungsbibliothek [D-GO1], Mus. pag. 14 d/7 ("Sonata pour le Piano-Forte avec l'accompagnement d'un Violon"). [Copyist piano part]

III   Vienna, Gesellschaft der Musikfreunde, MS Q 17754 ("Sonate pour le Pianoforte avec accompagnement d'un Violon"). [Copyist piano part]

IV   Vienna, Gesellschaft der Musikfreunde, MS Q 17757. [Copyist piano part and separate copyist violin part]

As noted in the discussion of the music, Archduke Rudolph's first draft of the violin sonata was drastically revised, as can be seen by a comparison of the autograph facsimile in Appendix 2 with the version printed here. The four manuscript copies, which appear to transmit a final version of the sonata, are substantially alike, but all of them contain numerous errors, made by the copyists, that differ from manuscript to manuscript. The most important and obvious errors concern notes or accidentals misplaced in the staves, while those of a minor nature affect slurs and dynamic indications.

The four manuscripts seem to fall into two pairs in their content: Sources I and II share similar errors, while sources III and IV share similar variants from I and II.

Since selection of one of these copies as a principal source seemed a fairly arbitrary matter, the editor decided to use the copy that offers the clearest and most consistent rendering of expression marks, source IV. The accompanying violin part of source IV, included with the piano part under the siglum Q 17757, is in a different hand than the piano part, and it is not clear how the two came to be cataloged together by archivists in the Gesellschaft der Musikfreunde. However, the violin part of IV is carefully written, and although not entirely free of errors, it is appropriate for use as a principal source. Any variants of a substantive nature existing in the other manuscripts are reported in the Critical Notes.

Editorial Methods

Forty Variations

The main editorial changes in the present edition involve minor modernizations of the text found in S, the principal source. Most affect only the layout of the score and not its musical content. As noted in The Sources, the first published edition closely corresponds to the two chief manuscript sources, Rudolph's final emended autograph (version II) and the copyist's manuscript, and the publication appears to reflect careful proofreading. The musical text of this edition generally follows that of the principal source; editorial procedures regarding changes are described below.

ACCIDENTALS

All accidentals missing in the principal source are given in brackets. Redundant accidentals have for the most part been eliminated; a few have been kept as cautionary accidentals. Editorial cautionary accidentals appear smaller than source accidentals.

DYNAMICS

A persistent problem in the principal source, usually owing to the cramped format, is the ambiguous placement of performance marks for dynamics (including crescendo and diminuendo signs) and accents. The two manuscript sources have been consulted for clarification of these ambiguities, and in most cases they have provided more accurate information for placement. Also problematical is the size of some accents, as well as their placement; in several places the editor has had to interpret these marks either as accents or hairpin diminuendos. Editorial hairpins use dashed lines.

The archduke's use, in general, of dynamic indications for loudness is itself often ambiguous. The use of *f*, for example, can indicate either a general dynamic level of *forte* or simply an accent. Similarly, the signs *fz*, *sf*, and *sfz* (and, at m. 182, a unique sign, *smfz*) are all used at various times for *sforzando* accents of varying intensities. These dynamic markings have been reproduced as the composer indicated them, and the performer should interpret them within the context of a given passage.

SLURS AND TIES

In the case of triplet and sextuplet groupings, Rudolph's practice is to indicate these groupettes simply with the appropriate number; if a curve is present, it represents a legato slur rather than a numerical grouping of notes. Another feature of the composer's orthography is his practice of omitting inner-voice ties in tied chords; he usually gives ties for the upper and lower voices only. In principal source S these ties are given inconsistently; editorial ties and slurs in the present edition appear as dashed curves.

BEAMS

Although the beaming in this edition generally follows that in primary source S, there are a few places where the composer's notation, as appears in A and G, differs in beaming and slurring from S. In those cases the autograph reading is preferred, and the reading in S is reported in the Critical Notes.

STACCATO

Rudolph's indications for staccato dots are consistent in his manuscripts, appearing somewhat elongated and a little like strokes. In primary source S the staccato dots appear throughout as wedges, with one exception, in measure 312, where dots are used on beats 3 and 4 in the lower staff. In the present edition, all staccatos appear as dots. A few articulation marks that were omitted from primary source S but that are found in both manuscript sources appear in brackets in this edition.

MISCELLANEOUS

Occasionally the stemming in S differs from that found in A; while generally following the stemming in S, this edition tacitly reverts to that in A when it proves more consistent. Editorial stems that appear in none of the sources are bracketed. For clarification of the part writing, some editorial rests, which appear smaller than source rests, have been added. Meter signs are those of the sources. Source double bar lines before changes of key that are not also sectional divisions are converted here to single bar lines. Other areas of modernization of principal source S include repositioning titles, metronome marks, dynamics, and expression indications. Abbreviations (e.g., *cres.*) have also been modernized. Pedal markings, which appear between the two staves in S, have been repositioned below the system.

Sonata in F Minor for Violin and Piano

The primary editorial procedure for the sonata consisted of writing out a score based on the principal source, source IV, correcting obvious errors made by the copyist such as misplaced accidentals, notes, or clef signs. In some instances variant readings in the other manuscript sources were preferable: when these are incorporated in the edition, the reading of the principal source is reported in the Critical Notes.

Redundant accidentals have been tacitly eliminated. Editorial emendations, including missing accidentals, articulation marks such as staccato dots, dynamic indications, or tempo changes, are enclosed in brackets. The editor has added slurs in many cases where parallel or adjacent passages suggest they were intended; these, along with editorial hairpins or ties, appear as dashed lines.

Ornament signs and appoggiaturas are given as they appear in the principal source. The copyist has carefully differentiated between trill signs and mordants in parallel passages (e.g., first movement, m. 17 and m. 163); the present edition follows the ornaments as they are given. It should be noted that the copyists of sources I and II treat the same ornament signs differently; they sometimes appear as short trills (⁓) or as turns (∽).

Beaming, which is consistent in all the manuscript copies, follows the principal source, as do meter signs. Source double bar lines before changes of key that are not also sectional divisions are converted to single bar lines.

The third movement Menuetto and its two Trios have been written out in full in this edition for easier reading, a procedure that does not appear in any of the sources. In sources III and IV, the Menuetto is followed by Trio I with a "menuetto da capo" instruction, then by Trio II, Menuetto again, and Coda. The violin part of source IV lacks the repeat of the Menuetto. Source I lacks any da capo signs, but the separate violin part has repeat signs. Finally, source II presents the Menuetto, the two Trios, and the Coda with da capo signs following each Trio.

As noted in The Sources, the separate violin part of source IV has served as the principal source for the present edition. The same editorial procedures used in the piano part apply to the violin part as it appears in the score.

For the performer's violin part supplementing this edition, the editor, Josef Suk, has prepared a performing edition that includes bowings, fingerings, articulation marks, and dynamics.

Critical Notes

Abbreviations for sources are given at the beginning of each set of critical notes. Simultaneous pitches appear separated by slashes (c/e/g), and read from the lowest note up; successive pitches are separated by commas (c, e, g). The identification of pitches follows the system wherein c' = middle C, c = the octave below middle C, c" = the octave above middle C, and so on. M(m). = the abbreviation for measure(s).

Forty Variations

References follow the source designations given in The Sources:

S Steiner publication (principal source)
A Autograph
G Manuscript copy

M. 42, decrescendo hairpin in A. M. 95, *sf* on beat 1 followed by a decrescendo hairpin in A and G. M. 96, slur in lower staff ends on beat 2 in A; in both staves, slur ends on beat 3 in G. M. 157, beat 4 is marked *f* in G. M. 174, beat 3 is marked *pp* in A and G. M. 186, editorial *crescendo* follows A and G. M. 189, lower staff, beats 1 and 2 are beamed together, beats 3 and 4 are beamed together—edition follows A. M. 190, lower staff, beats 1 and 2 are beamed together—edition follows A. M. 194, decrescendo hairpin in A and G. Mm. 203, 204, 205, 206, sforzando markings appear below grace notes: in A and G, they appear beneath main notes—edition follows A and G; grace notes in these measures appear variously with eighth or sixteenth flags, some with slashes—edition follows A, where all grace notes uniformly have eighth flags with slashes. M. 206, lower staff, beat 2, chord lacks *fz*—edition follows A. M. 225 crescendo hairpin to *fz* on beat 3 follows A and G. M. 226, beats 2–3, editorial hairpins follow A and G.

Mm. 339–60 (var. 38), grace notes uniformly have sixteenth flags, in mm. 350 and 360 with a slash—edition follows A, where all grace notes have eighth flags with a slash. M. 366, upper staff, editorial slur follows A and G. Mm. 369–70, editorial hairpin follows A and G. M. 393, upper staff, note 1, editorial flat follows A and G. M. 394, upper staff, note 1, editorial flat follows A and G; lower staff, half note in bass lacks dot. M. 395, lower staff, half note in bass lacks dot.

M. 425, editorial *f* follows A and G. M. 430, editorial *p* on the anacrusis to m. 431 follows A and G. M. 471, upper staff, beat 1, top note (a" of chord) lacks dot. M. 524, upper staff, editorial slur follows A. M. 527, upper staff, beat 3 has a" only—edition follows A and G. M. 542, editorial *f* follows A and G.

M. 603, upper staff, beat 1, d' of upper-voice dyad lacks dot. M. 604, upper staff, beat 1, e' of upper-voice dyad lacks dot. M. 649, upper staff, editorial slur follows A and G. Mm. 656–57, crescendo extender dashes end at m. 656, beat 4—edition follows A and G. M. 665, beat 4, alto voice is d'—edition follows A (where Beethoven changed the original pitch of f'-sharp to e') and G.

M. 700, editorial hairpin follows A and G. M. 738, upper staff, lower voice, dyad is e"/(unsharped) g'—edition follows A and G.

Sonata in F Minor for Violin and Piano

References to the sources follow the enumeration given under The Sources:

I   full score and separate violin part
II piano part only
III piano part only
IV piano part and separate violin part

References are for the piano part, unless specifically indicated for the violin. The meter of the last movement of the sonata is *alla breve* (𝄵); for convenience of reference, the beats in each measure are counted as if in **C** (four quarter notes to a measure).

ALLEGRO

M. 4, violin, editorial slur on beat 1 follows I (score). M. 5, upper staff, beat 1, chord reads B-flat/d'-flat/b'-flat in I and II (cf. m. 164). M. 6, violin, editorial slur on last three notes follows I (score). M. 9, violin, beat 1 has *tr* ornament—edition follows I. M. 20, lower staff, beat 2, editorial E follows parallel m. 165. M. 32, violin, beat 2 is c"—edition follows I. M. 37, upper staff, beat 3, note 1 is d" in all sources—edition follows parallel m. 182. M. 38, treble clef sign added in lower staff for two mm. M. 62, upper staff, lowest note in chord is e'-flat in III and IV—edition follows I and II. M. 63, upper staff, beats 3–4, chords 1–3 have b-flat as lowest note—edition follows I and II. M. 69, violin, editorial slurs follow I. M. 70, upper staff, beat 3, natural sign before b missing. M. 75, lower staff, e-flat missing from chord.

M. 102, lower staff, beat 2, lower voice has d'-flat—edition follows I, II, and III. M. 122, violin, editorial *dolce* follows I. M. 130, violin, editorial *p* follows I. M. 158, upper staff, chord reads f'/a'-flat/c"/e"-natural in all sources. M. 180, violin, chord lacking in all sources—edition follows parallel in m. 35. M. 181, lower staff, beat 1 has c in all sources. M. 182, violin, editorial crescendo hairpin follows I. M. 195, violin, editorial slur follows I. Mm. 256–57, lower staff, editorial ties follow I and II.

ADAGIO

M. 24, violin has [rhythm figure]—edition follows I (score). M. 40, key signature changes to five flats in the middle of the measure, where source changes to next system (III changes to five flats at m. 41, also with the start of a new system)—edition follows I and II. M. 46, upper staff, beat 1, note 3 lacks natural. M. 51, upper staff, beat 1, note 3 is d-natural in all sources—the editor prefers d-flat to avoid a dissonant clash. M. 55, violin has *pp* on beat 2—edition moves dynamic to m. 56 to follow decrescendo hairpin and to align with piano part. M. 57, key change lacking in all sources (not needed in III and IV—see report for m. 40). M. 73, new key signature has four sharps in all sources.

MENUETTO

M. 10, upper staff, beat 1, lowest note (b) has natural. M. 49, violin, note 1 is written as e'-sharp. M. 51, lower staff, beat 2, note 1 is e-flat—edition follows I. M. 59, violin, editorial tie follows I. Mm. 259 and 262, violin, beat 1, grace notes lacking—edition follows I.

ALLEGRO ASSAI QUASI PRESTO

Tempo indication given as "Allegro assai più presto" in III and IV and in score of I—edition follows tempo indication in I (violin part) and II.

M. 59, lower staff, note is e-flat in all sources. M. 63, upper staff, beat 3 has c''' in all sources. M. 65, lower staff, beat 1, note 1 is B$_1$-flat—edition's D-flat is suggested by the parallel passage at m. 310. M. 83, upper staff, note 2 has a natural in all sources (note 6 also has a natural in II only). M. 91, upper staff, note 2 (b") has a natural. M. 107, violin, note 2 (b') lacks a natural. M. 121, upper staff, beat 1 has c". M. 141, upper staff, note 2 (b") has a flat sign in III and IV—edition follows I and II.

M. 204, upper staff, beat 4, note 1 is d'''—edition follows I and II. M. 217, pedal in III and IV. M. 241, lower staff, beat 3, note 2 is f. M. 244, lower staff, dyad is d'-flat/g'-flat in all sources. M. 252, violin, key change lacking. M. 289, upper staff, flat sign misplaced before a' in all sources.

Notes

1. Leopold succeeded his brother Joseph as emperor upon the latter's death in 1790, ruling for just two years before his own death in 1792. For full biographical details on Archduke Rudolph's life and works, see Susan Kagan, *Archduke Rudolph, Beethoven's Patron, Pupil, and Friend: His Life and Music* (Stuyvesant, N.Y.: Pendragon Press, 1988).

2. According to Anton Schindler, Beethoven's early biographer, Beethoven wrote the piano part of the Concerto for Piano, Violin, and Violoncello, op. 56 ("Triple" Concerto) with Rudolph in mind. See Anton Schindler, *Beethoven As I Knew Him*, ed. Donald W. MacArdle, trans. Constance S. Jolly (New York: W. W. Norton, 1972).

3. The two works are a Divertissement and a set of variations for czakan, or csákány (a cane flute of Hungarian origin), and piano. Archduke Rudolph did not put dates on any other compositions; a chronology of his oeuvre, established through various means such as handwriting, watermarks, and his own catalog entries, can be found in the thematic catalog (app. 3) of Kagan, *Archduke Rudolph*.

4. Archduke Rudolph pursued a lifelong interest in the fine arts and was apparently a talented copper engraver and painter. Although none of his art works can be found today, references in his correspondence, his will, and information from his catalogs document his work in this field. He also

maintained some business interests, being one of the founders of an iron works in an area of present-day Czechoslovakia.

5. Although nothing in his will specified a separation in his collection, his own compositions remained behind in the Kremsier palace library.

6. There are isolated copies of Rudolph's work in the Landesbibliothek in Gotha and in the Thüringische Landesbibliothek in Weimar.

7. The purpose of Diabelli's project was a publication celebrating Austrian musical talent (including among its contributors the fourteen-year-old Franz Liszt). His solicitation of a contribution from Archduke Rudolph, well-known as Beethoven's patron and pupil in Vienna, was undoubtedly both patriotic and politic, but at the same time it served to recognize Rudolph's status as a composer.

8. Although the Sonata in A for Clarinet and Piano was not published until 1824, handwriting features of the autograph suggest that it was composed approximately at the same time as the Sonata for Violin and Piano.

9. A facsimile of the Beethoven autograph is reproduced in Kagan, *Archduke Rudolph,* pl. 24.

10. See Emily Anderson, *The Letters of Beethoven,* vol. 2 (New York: St. Martin's Press, 1961).

11. *Allgemeine musikalische Zeitung* 22 (19 January 1820): cols. 33–41; *Allgemeine musikalische Zeitung mit besonderer Rücksicht auf den österreichischen Kaiserstaat* 4 (10 June 1820): cols. 369–75.

12. Archduke Rudolph's procedure in the opening—an Adagio in G Minor followed by a folklike melody in G major—bears a striking resemblance to Beethoven's *Variations on "Ich bin der Schneider Kakadu" for Piano, Violin, and Cello,* op. 121a. Although not published until 1823, the "Kakadu" Variations had been composed seven years earlier.

13. Two copies of the Steiner print (*Wgm* Q 15076, Q 11428), one of which had been in Brahms's possession, are in the Gesellschaft der Musikfreunde. Another copy is in the Musiksammlung der Österreichische Nationalbibliothek in Vienna (MS 36576). An abridged version of the variations—comprising original numbers 1–6, 10–16, 19–20, 23, 25, 31–36 (the last reduced to eight measures), 38, and the fugue only of 40—with fingerings by Beethoven, was published in 1821 by Friedrich Starke in his didactic series of piano works, the Wiener-Piano-Forte-Schule. The extent of Rudolph's direct participation in the abridgment, if any, is unknown.

14. Although the variations can be played at the tempos indicated by the metronome markings, they are exceedingly fast. For discussion of the metronome during this period and questions of tempo in Beethoven's music, see William S. Newman, *Beethoven on Beethoven: Playing His Piano Music His Way* (New York: W. W. Norton, 1988).

15. When Rudolph's collection was first cataloged in Kroměříž, the archivists apparently failed to recognize the relationship between the slow movement and the other three movements and cataloged it as a separate composition.

Plate 1. CS-KRa A 4375, [page 6], unpaginated: Beethoven's suggested title for the *Forty Variations*.

FORTY VARIATIONS
ON A THEME BY BEETHOVEN

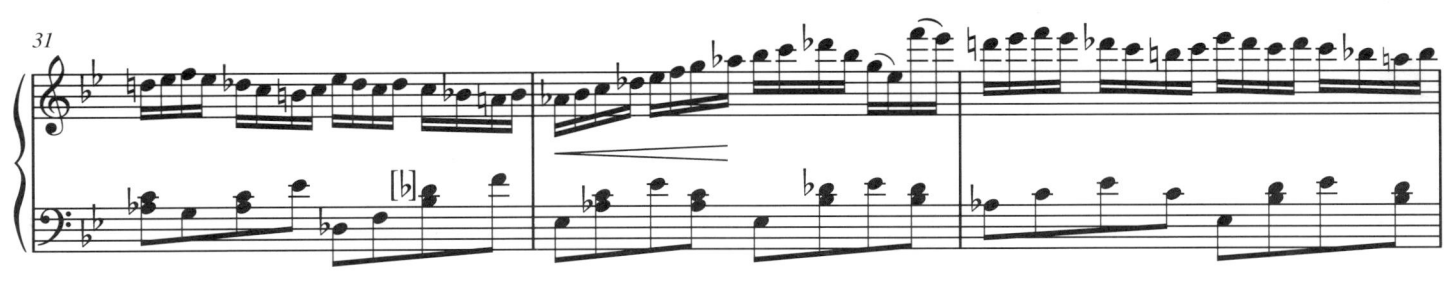

4

Var. 37

Tempo di marcia (♩ = 104)

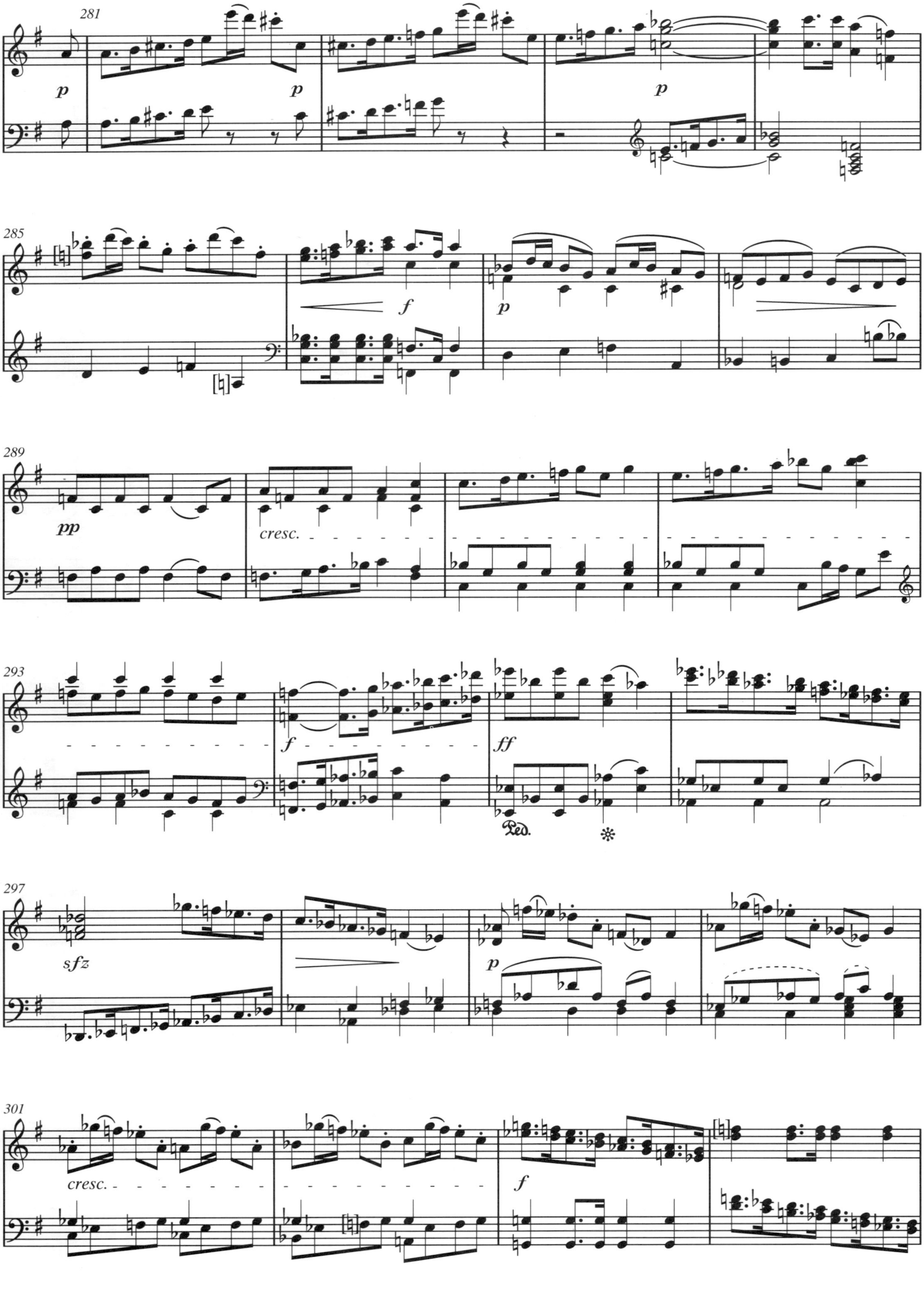
281
p
p
p
285
f
p
289
pp
cresc.
293
f
ff
Ped.
297
sfz
p
301
cresc.
f

21

Var. 38

Allegro molto (𝅝 = 108)

Var. 39

Tempo di Menuetto (♩ = 126)

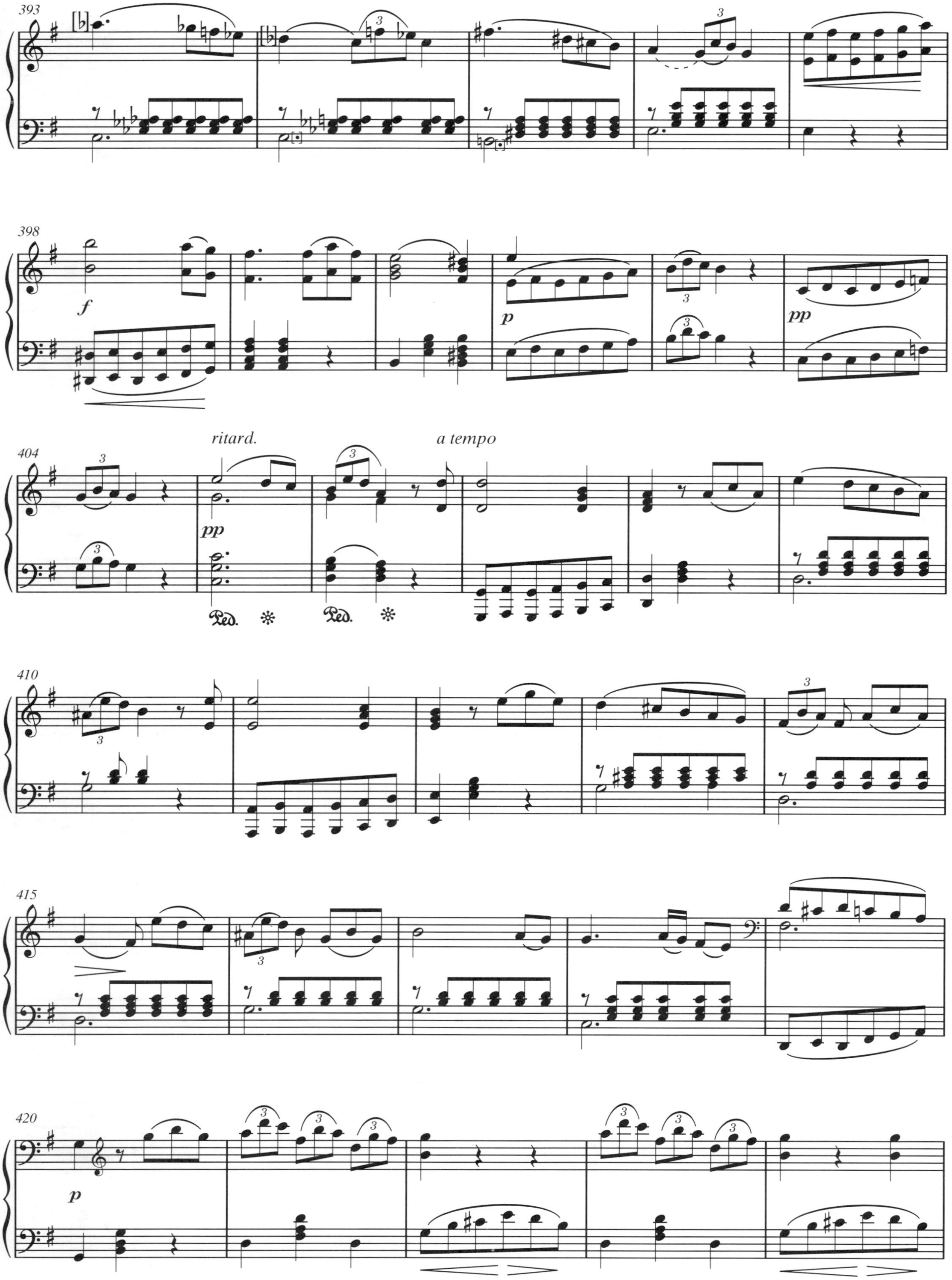
393
398
f
p
pp
404
ritard.
a tempo
pp
Ped.
Ped.
410
415
420
p

Var. 40. Finale

Allegro agitato (♩ = 104)

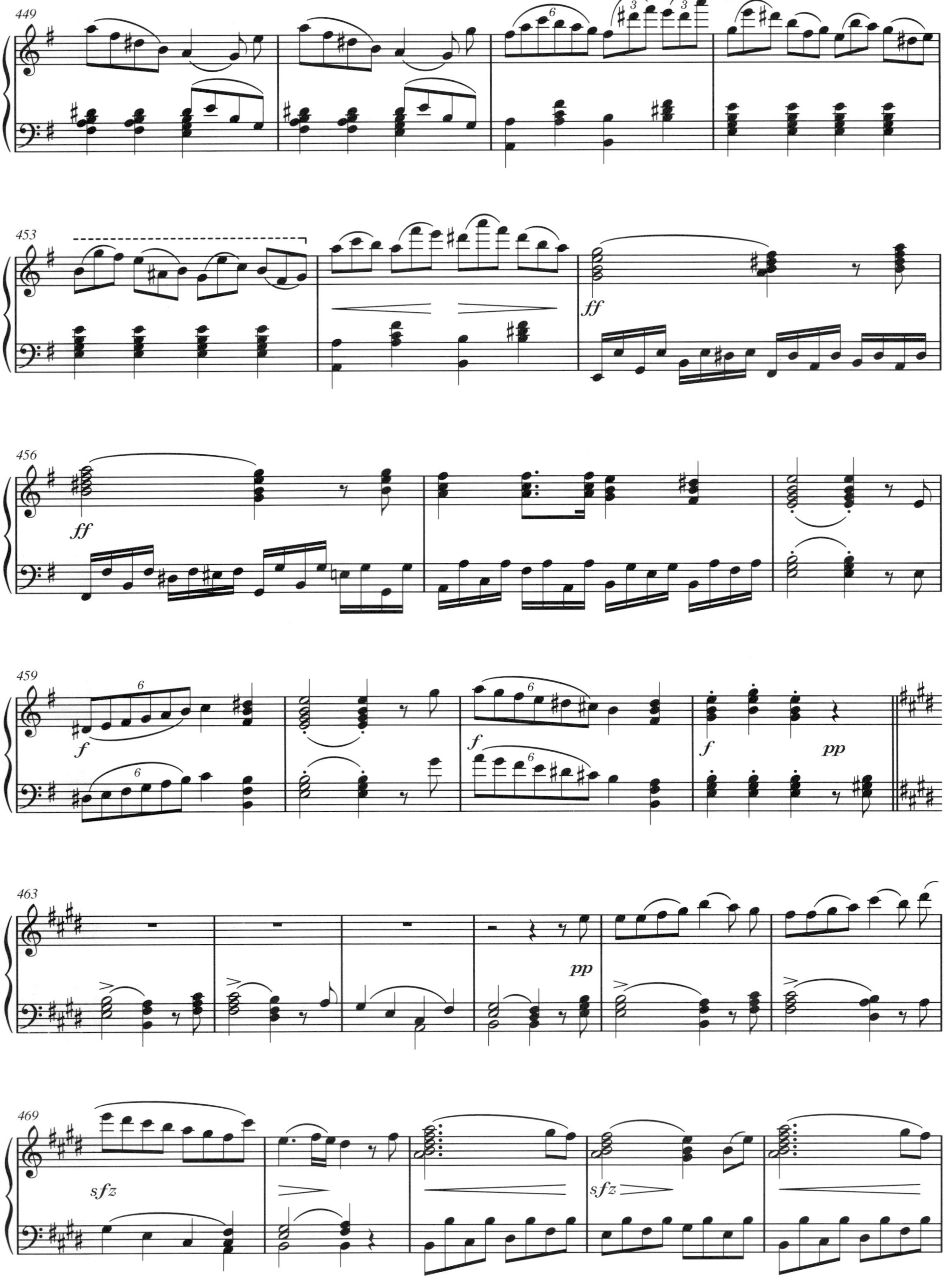
449
8va
453
ff
456
ff
459
f
f
f
pp
463
pp
469
sfz
sfz

27

28

521
f
f
ff
525
f
[f]
6
sfz
528
8va
6
6
cresc.
532
3
3
f
535
ff
ff
f
538
6
f
f
6
[f]

543
p
p
548
p
553
sfz
sfz
cresc.
558
sfz
sfz
f
p
563
f
f
fz
fz
sfz
decresc.
568
p

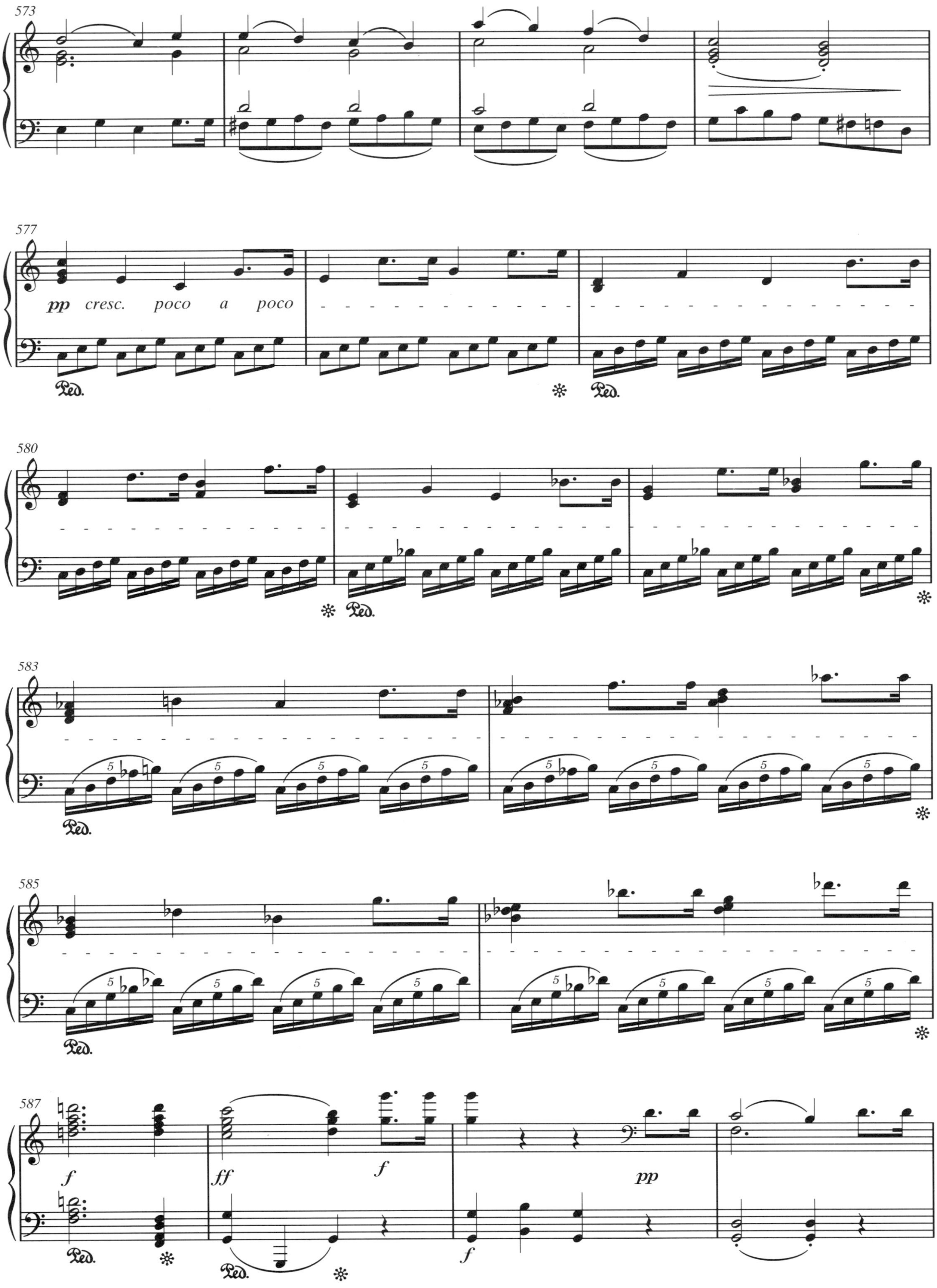
573
577
pp cresc. poco a poco
Ped.
580
583
585
587
f
ff
f
pp
f

591
cresc. poco a poco
594
f
ff
ff
p
598
f
p
cresc.
602
607
f
ff
pp
612
pp

618
f
621
f
ff
dim.
pp
p
625
Più Allegro (𝅗𝅥 = 120)
fz
fz
629
cresc.
f
f
633
p
f
636
f
ff
f

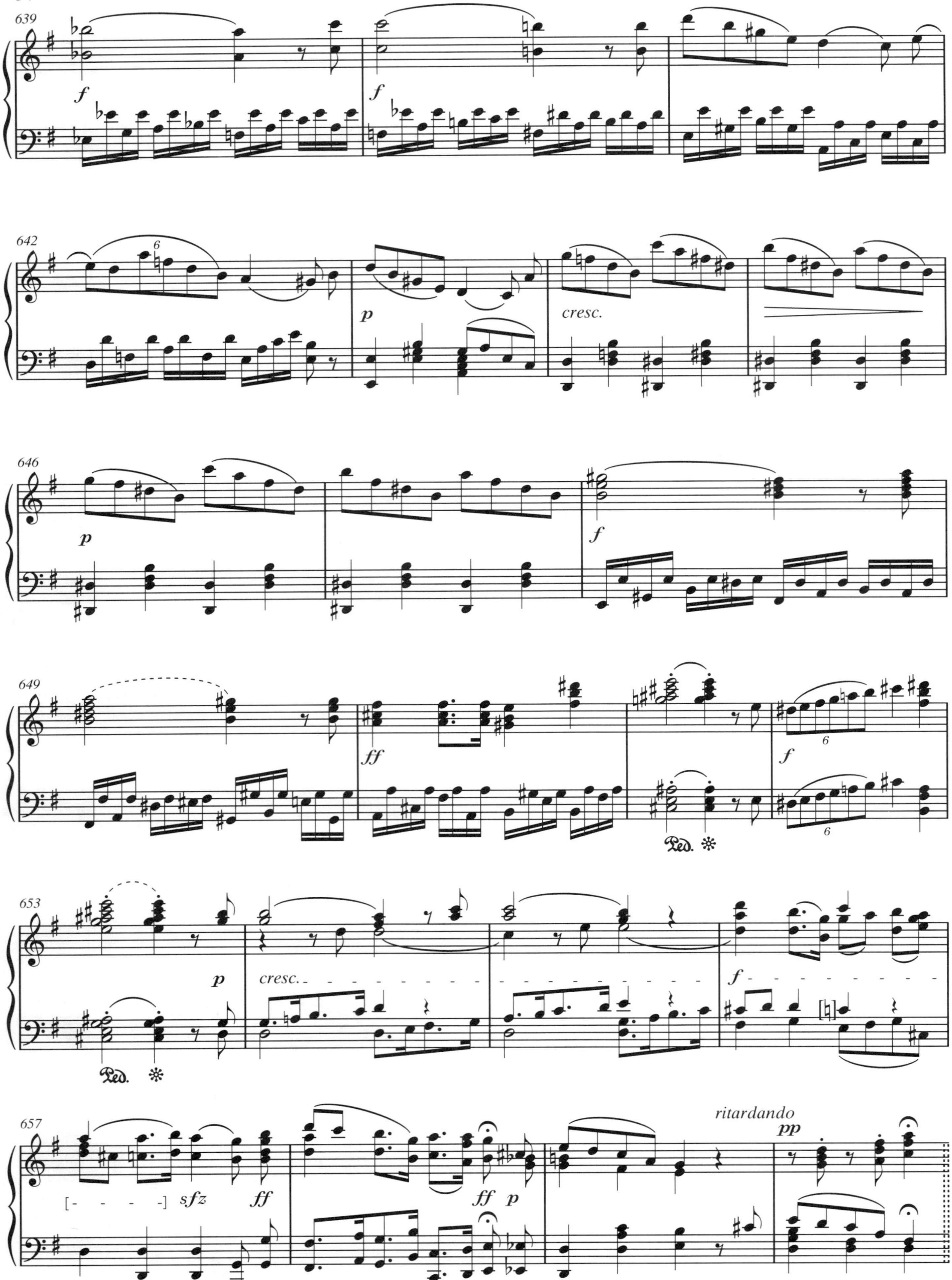
639
642
cresc.
646
649
ff
Ped.
653
cresc.
657
sfz
ritardando
pp

Allegro moderato assai (♩ = 152)
661
p
fz
666
p
670
674
fz
sfz
678
sf
682
sfz
p

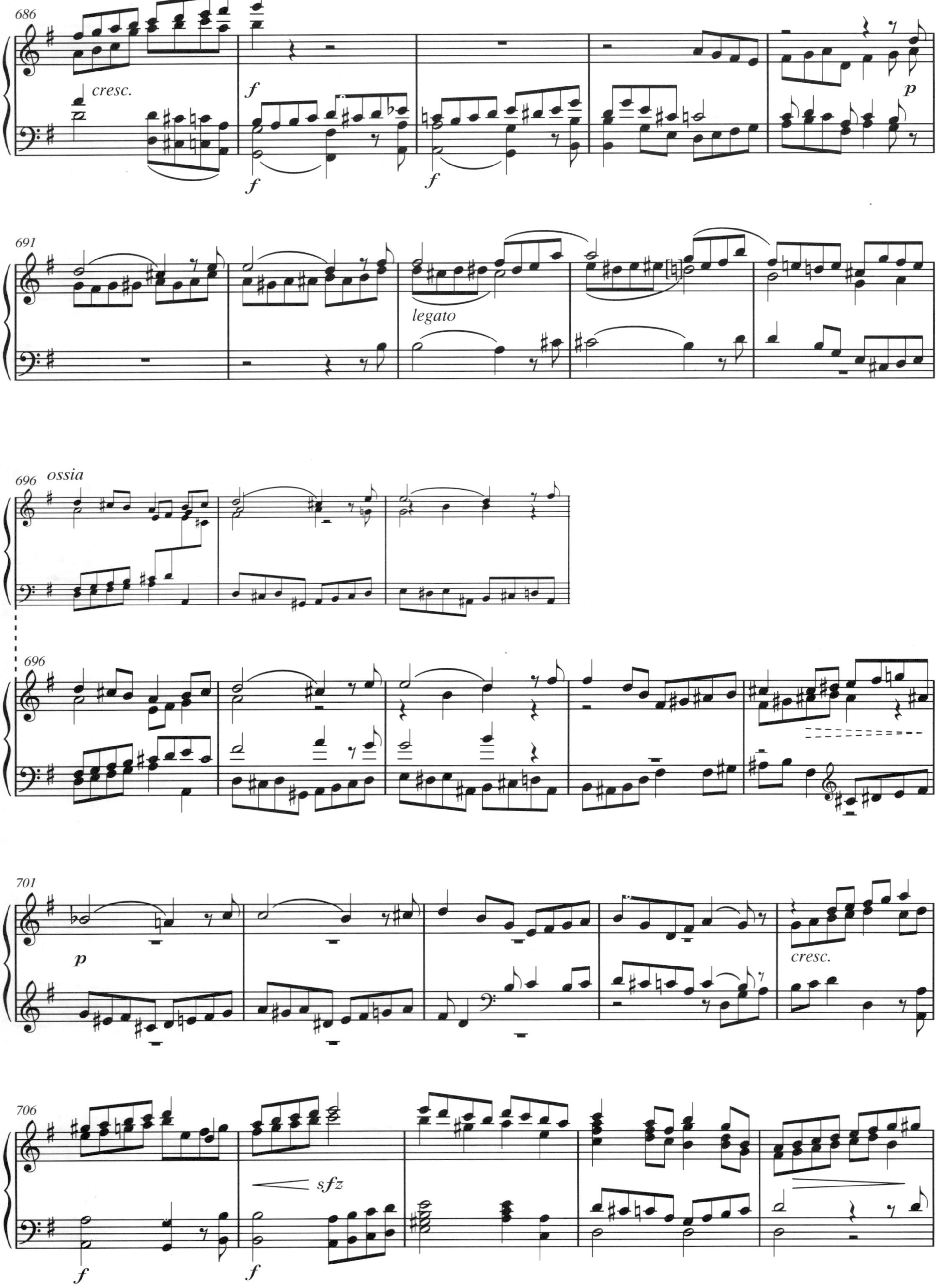
686
cresc.
f
f
f
p
691
legato
696
ossia
696
701
p
cresc.
706
sfz
f
f

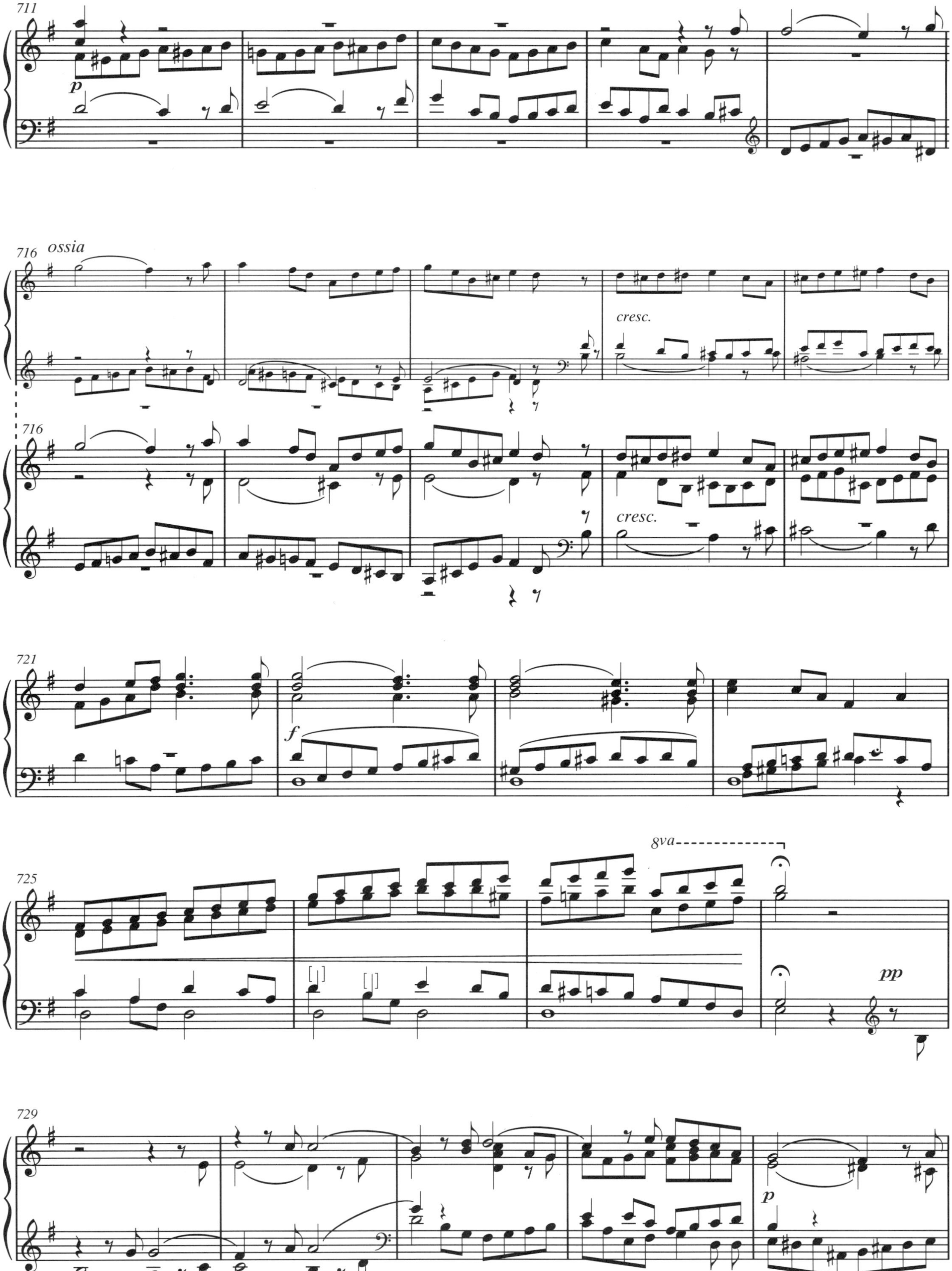
711
p
716
ossia
cresc.
716
cresc.
721
f
725
8va
pp
729
p

734
fz
cresc.
738
743
747
tr
p cresc.
f
752
8va
Adagio
ff
p
dim.
Ped.
Ped.
Ped.

SONATA IN F MINOR
FOR VIOLIN AND PIANO

41

42

43

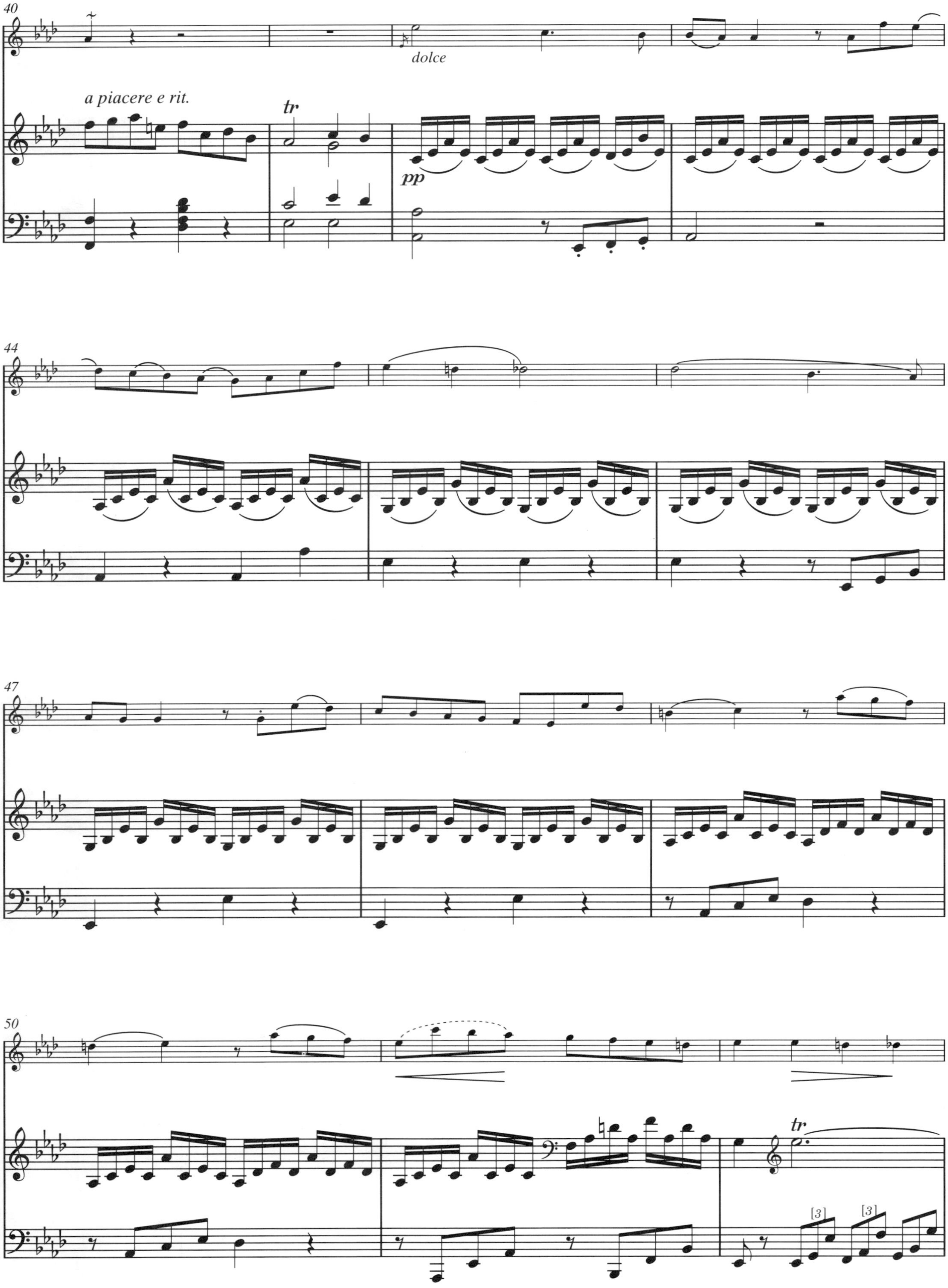
40
dolce
a piacere e rit.
tr
pp
44
47
50
tr
[3]
[3]

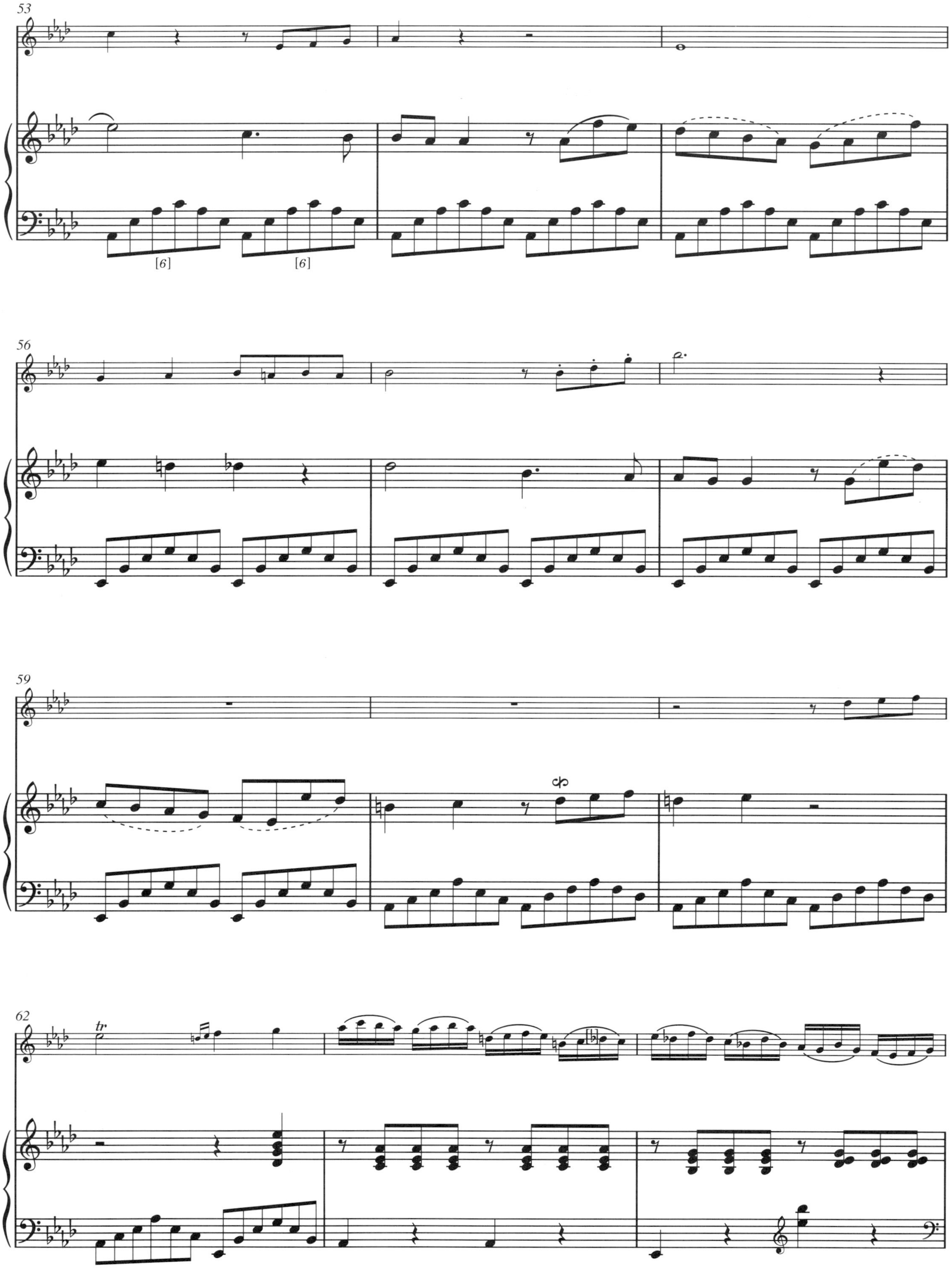
53
[6]
[6]
56
59
62
tr

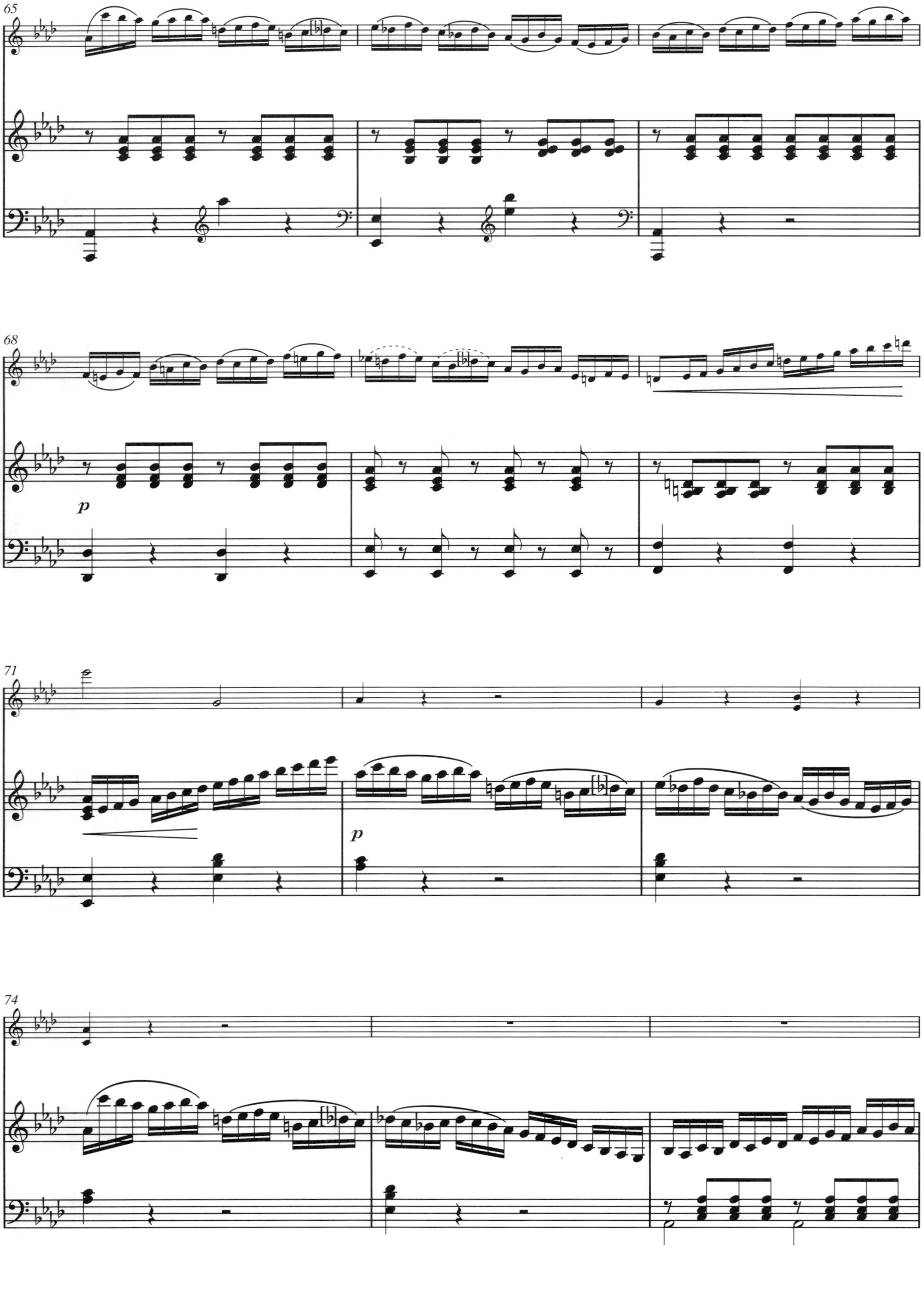
65
68
71
74

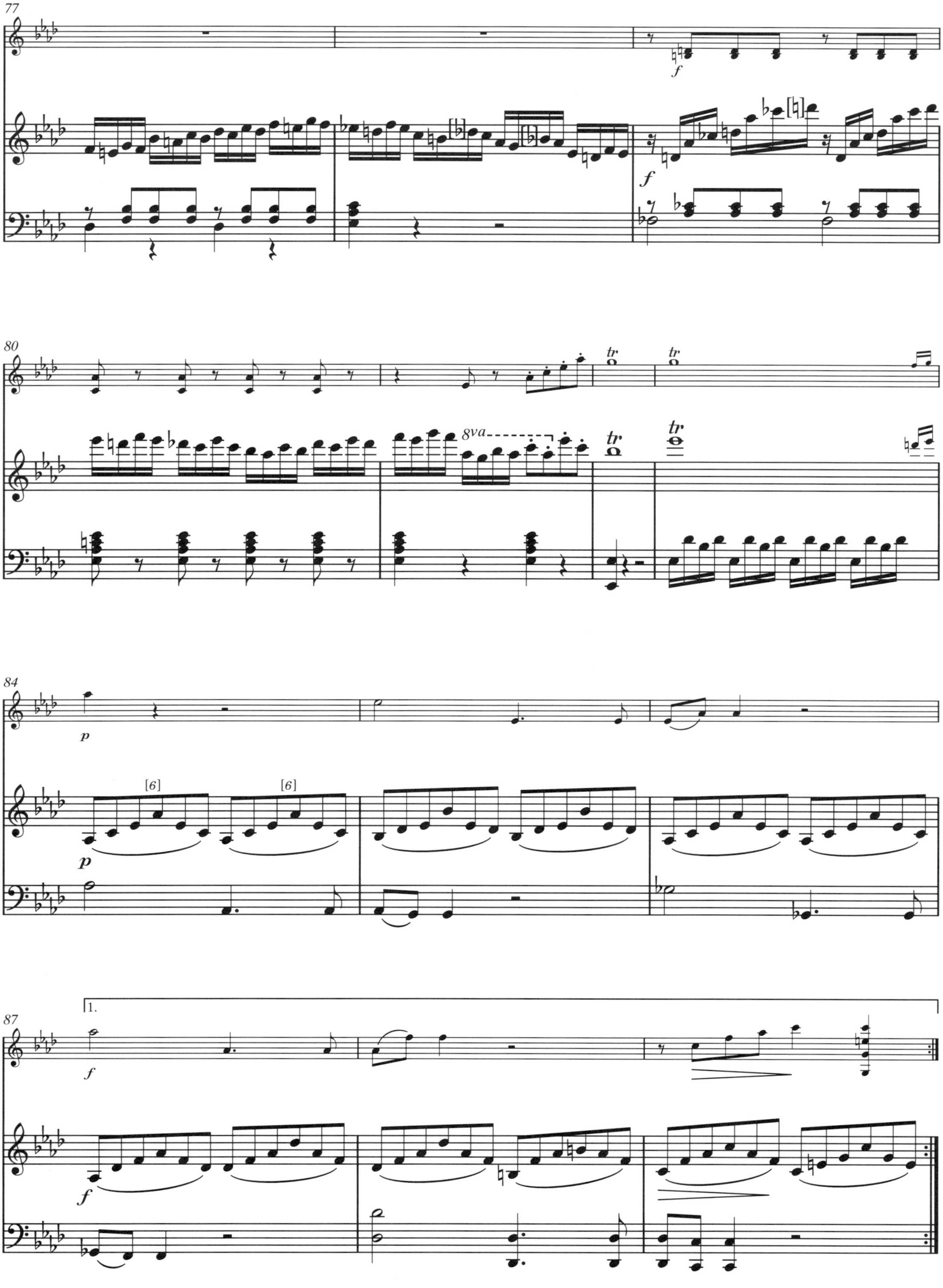
77
f
f
80
tr
tr
8va
tr
tr
84
p
[6]
[6]
p
87
1.
f
f

48

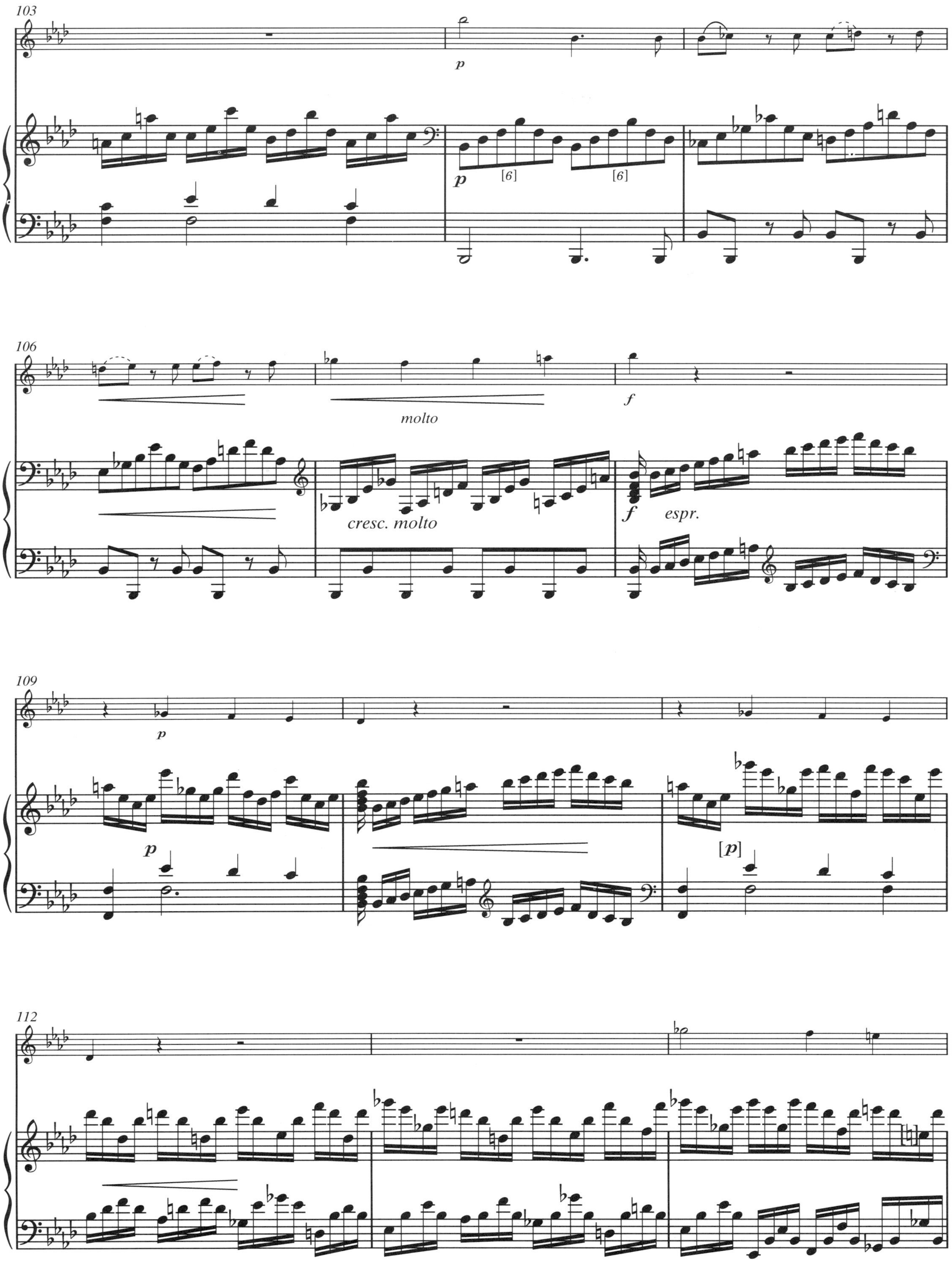
103
p
p
[6]
[6]
106
molto
cresc. molto
f
f
espr.
109
p
p
[p]
112

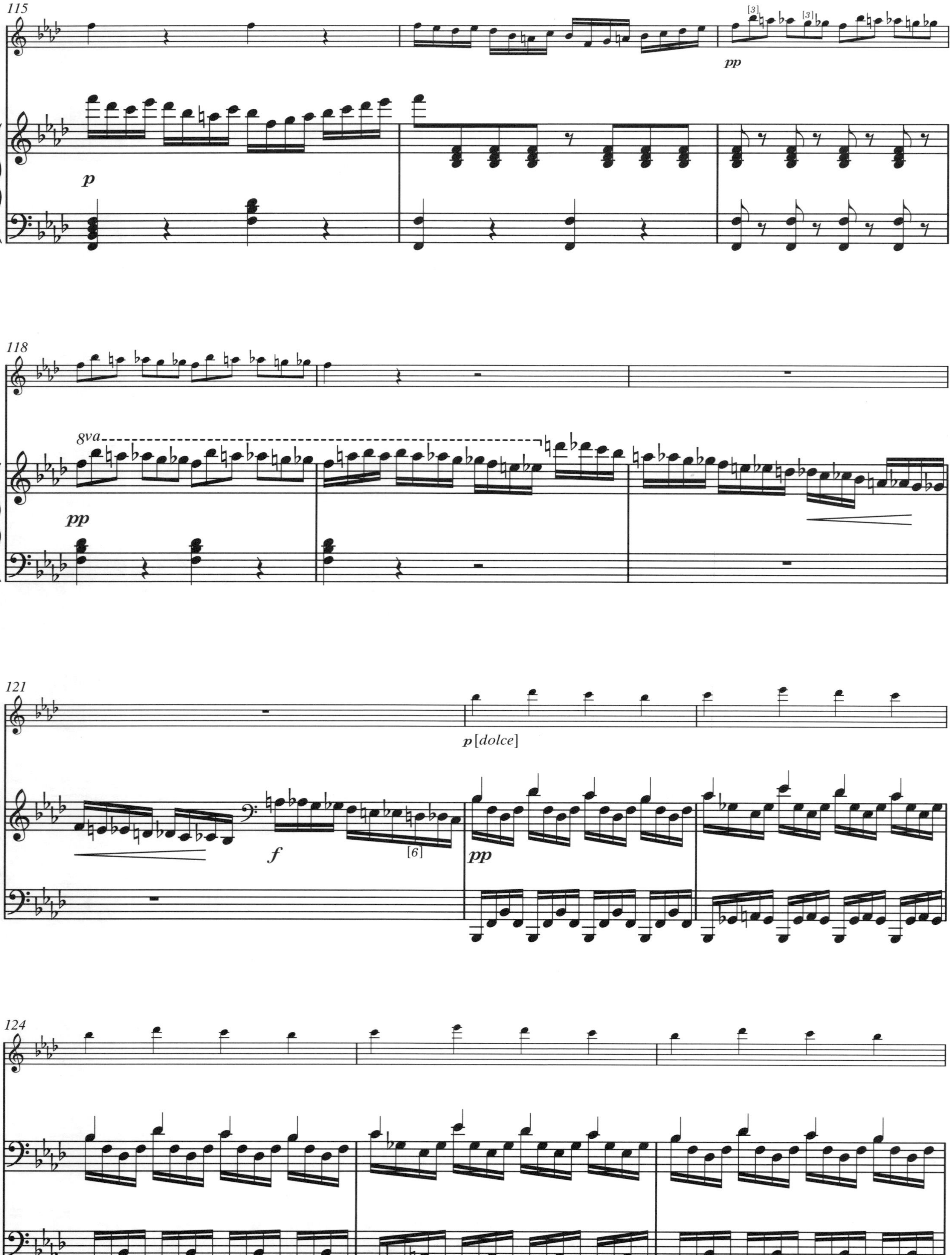
115
[3]
[3]
pp
p
118
8va
pp
121
f
[6]
p [dolce]
pp
124

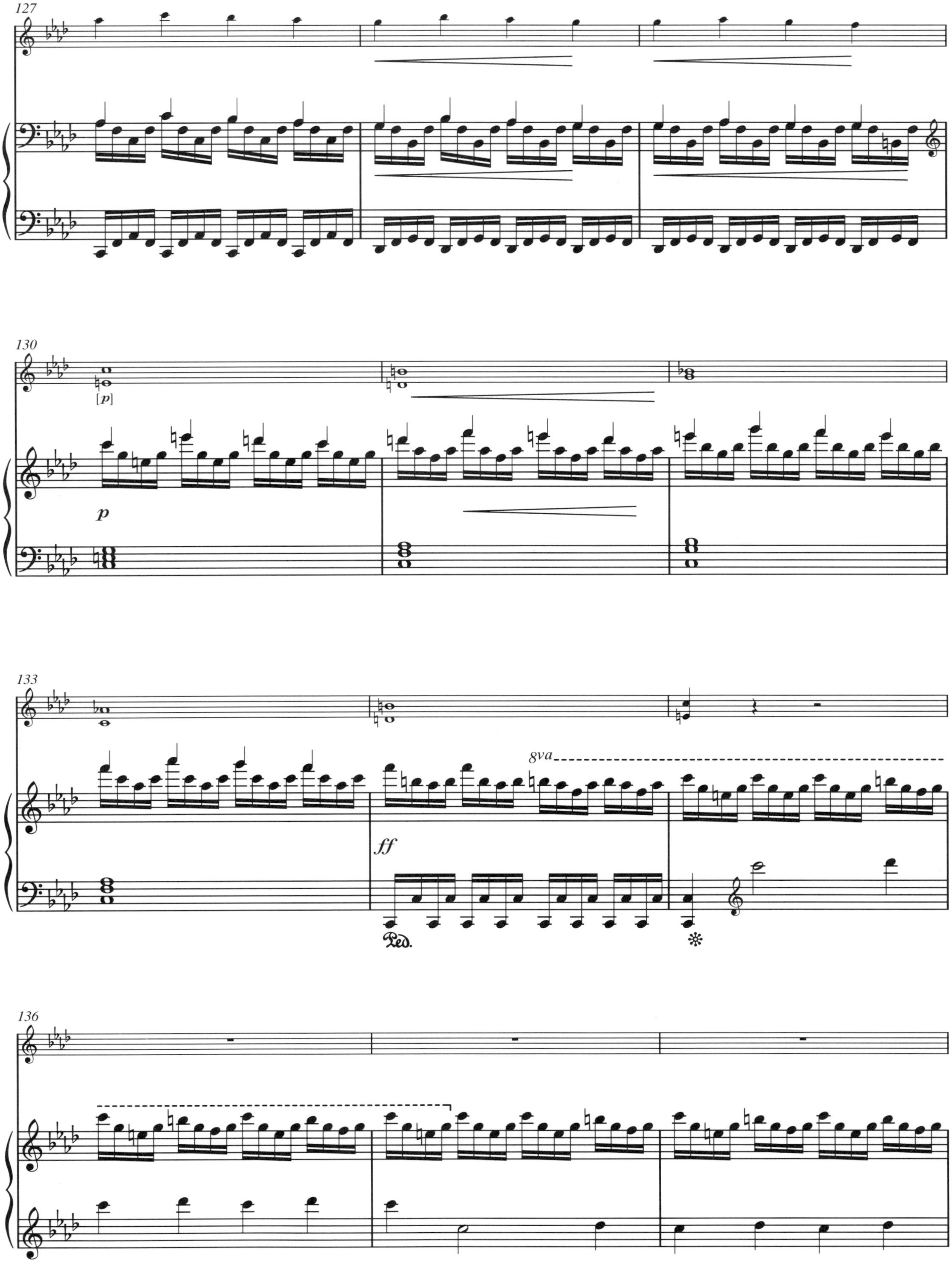
127
130
[p]
p
133
8va
ff
Ped.
136

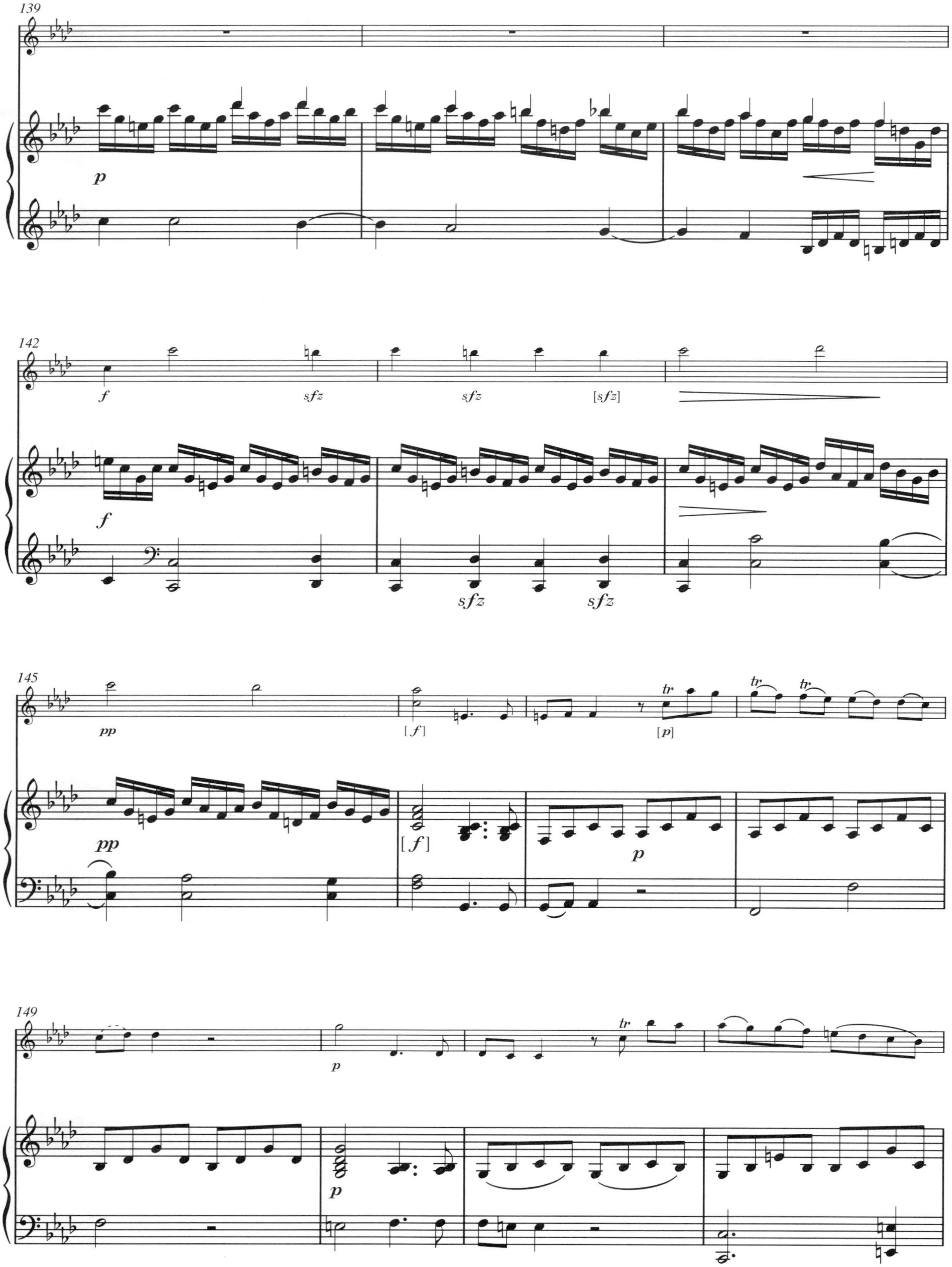
139
p
142
f
sfz
sfz
[sfz]
f
sfz
sfz
145
pp
[f]
tr
[p]
tr
tr
pp
[f]
p
149
p
tr
p

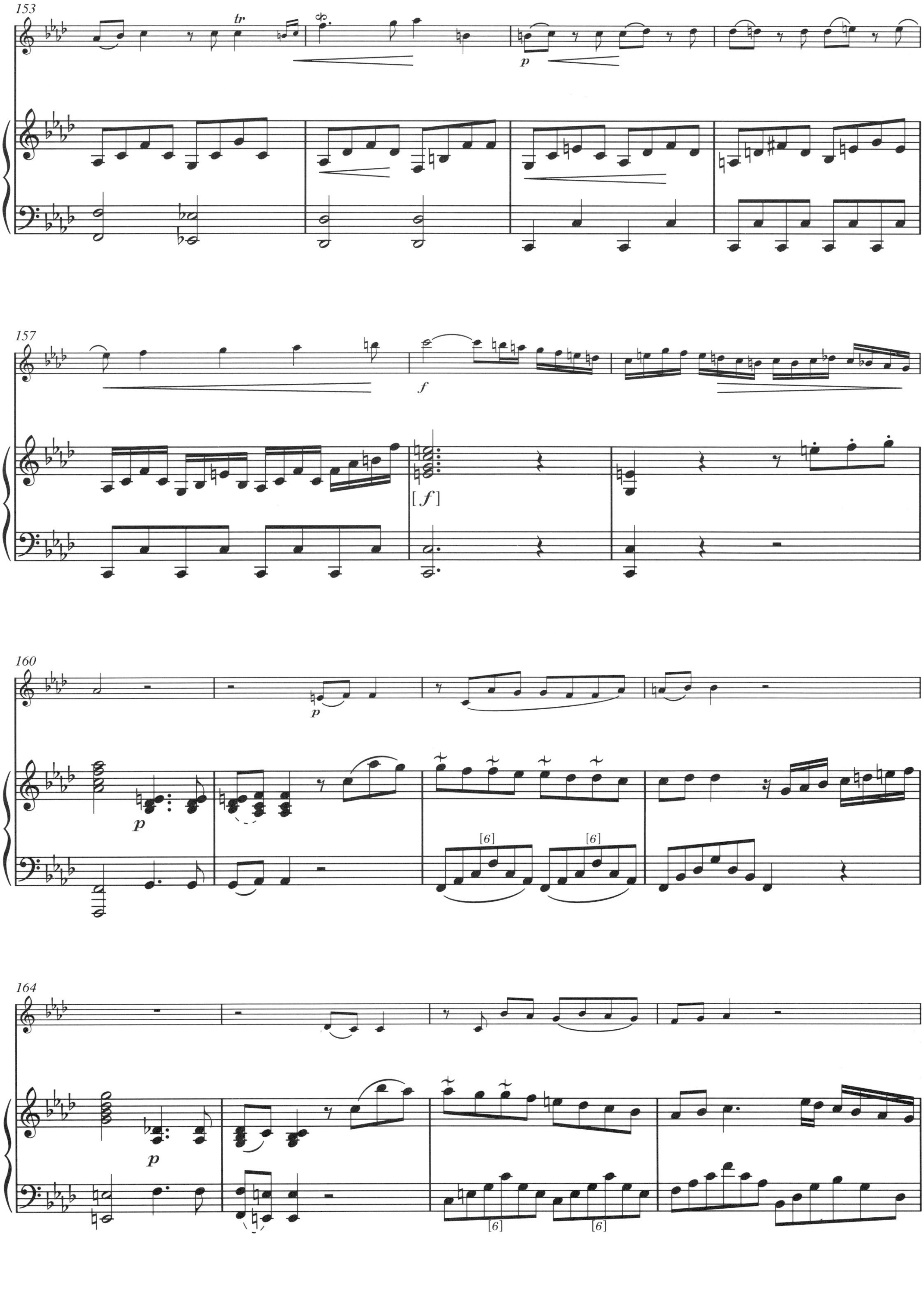
153
tr
p
157
f
[f]
160
p
p
[6]
[6]
164
p
[6]
[6]

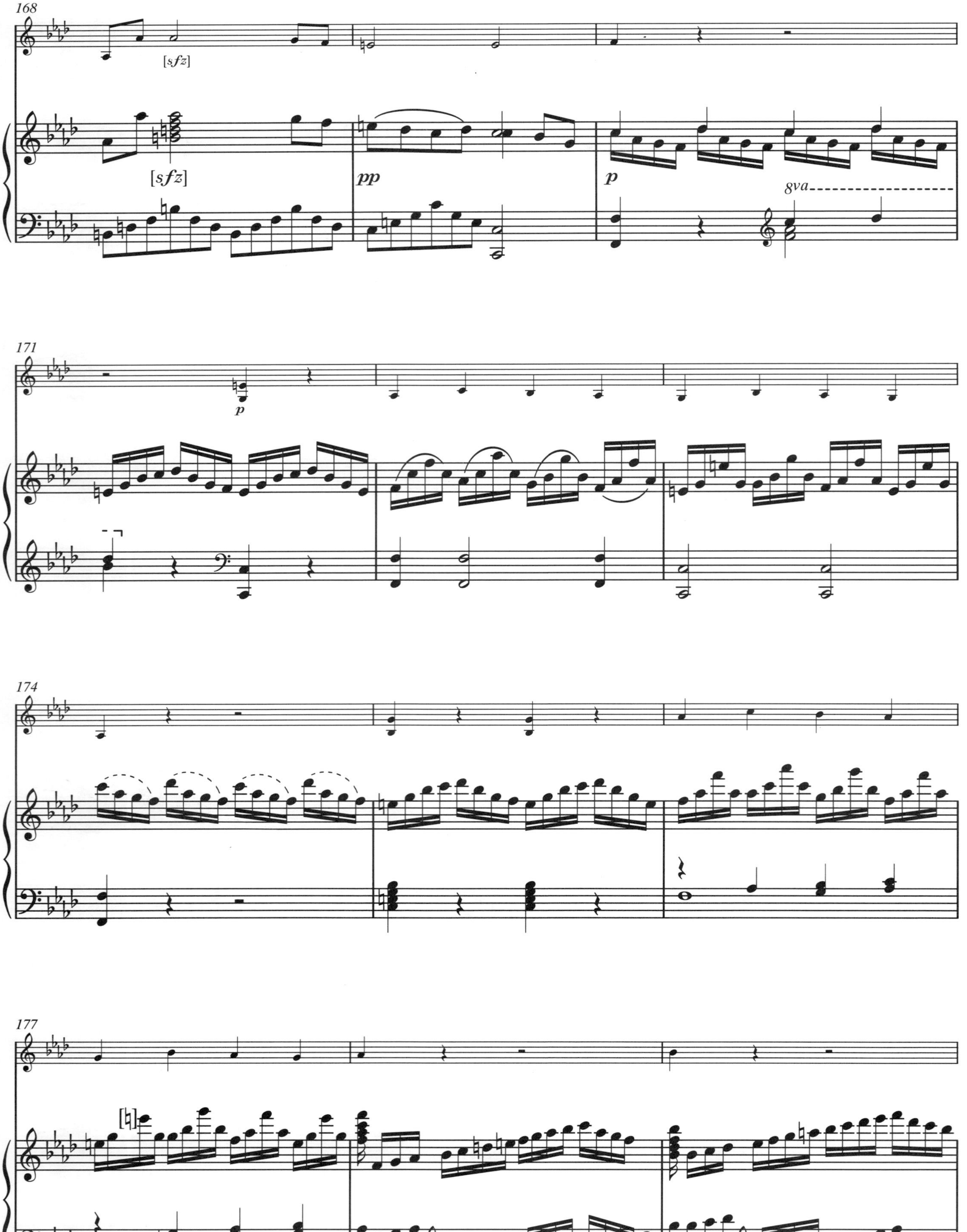
168
[sfz]
[sfz]
pp
p
8va
171
p
174
177

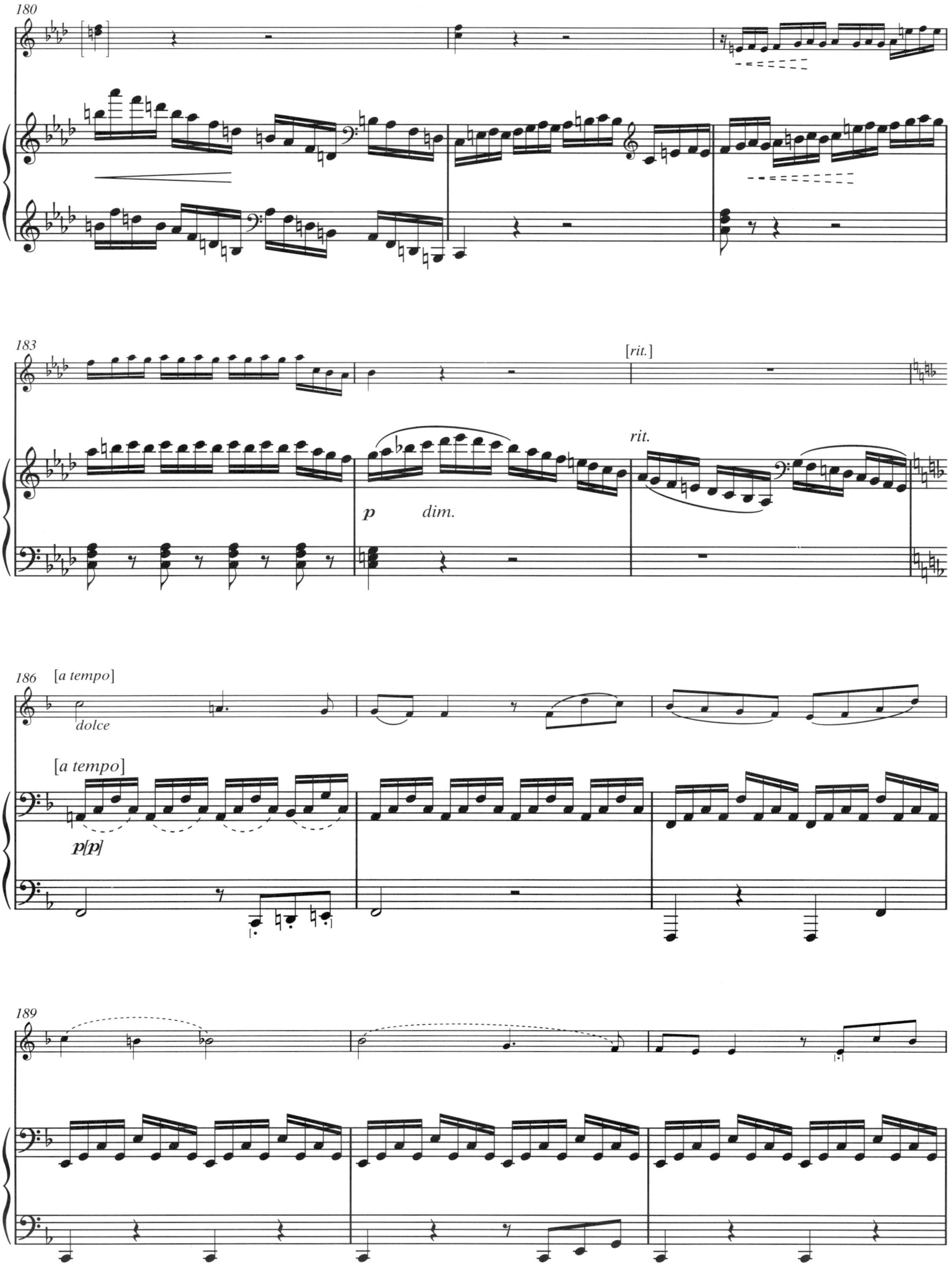
180
183
[rit.]
rit.
p
dim.
186
[a tempo]
dolce
[a tempo]
p[p]
189

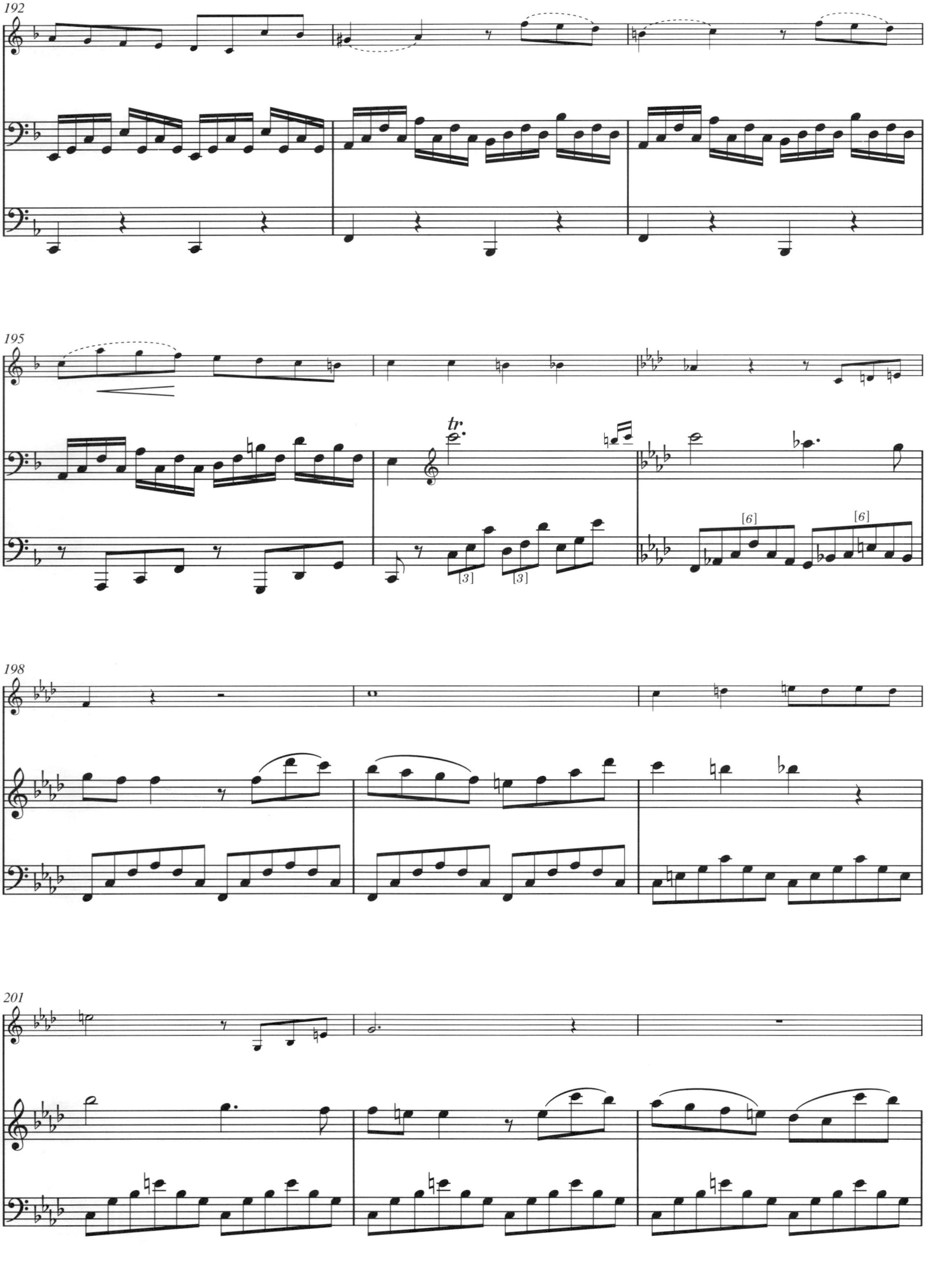
192
195
tr.
[6]
[6]
[3]
[3]
198
201

57

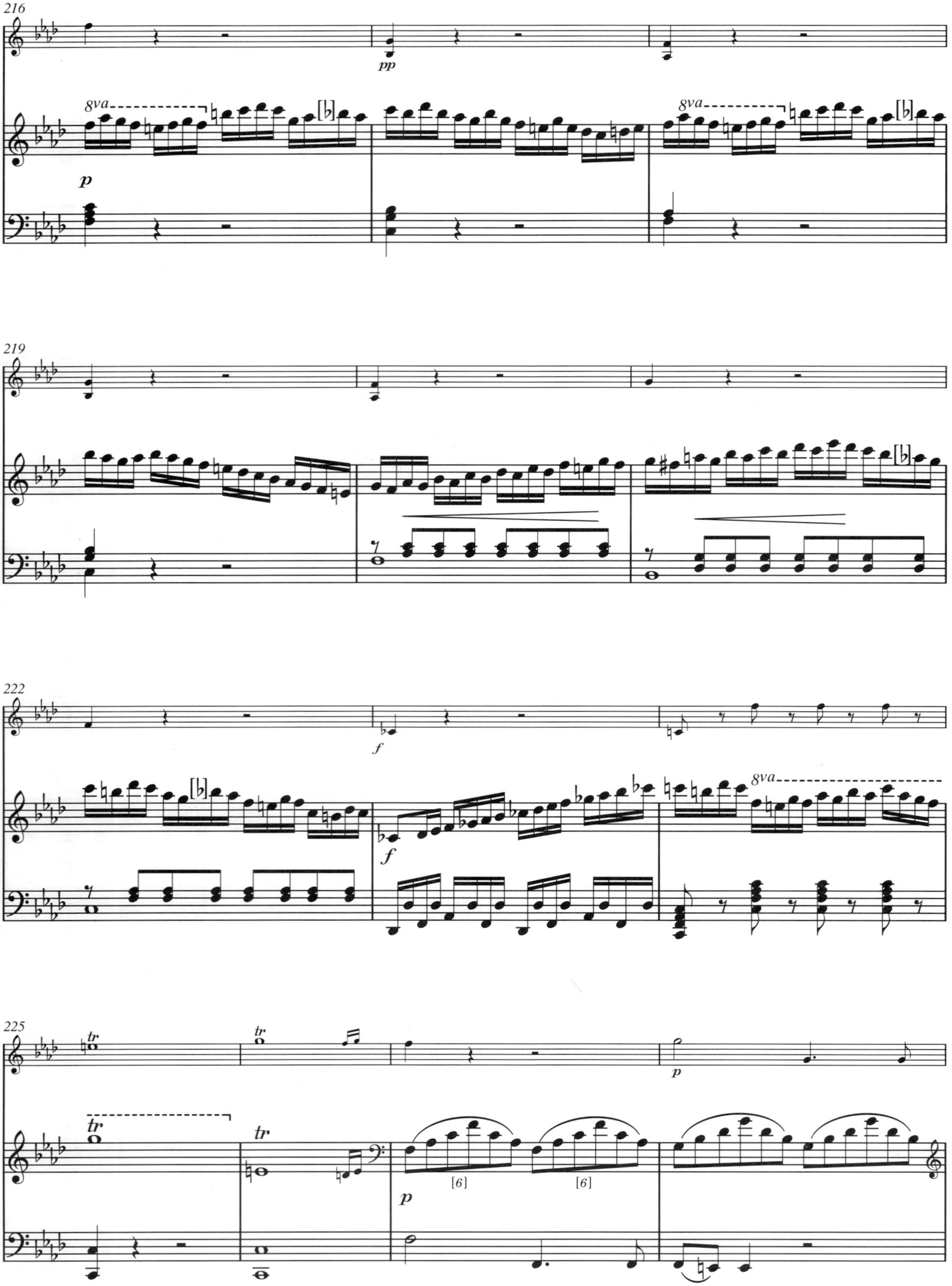
216
pp
8va
p
8va
219
222
f
f
8va
225
tr
tr
tr
tr
p
p
[6]
[6]

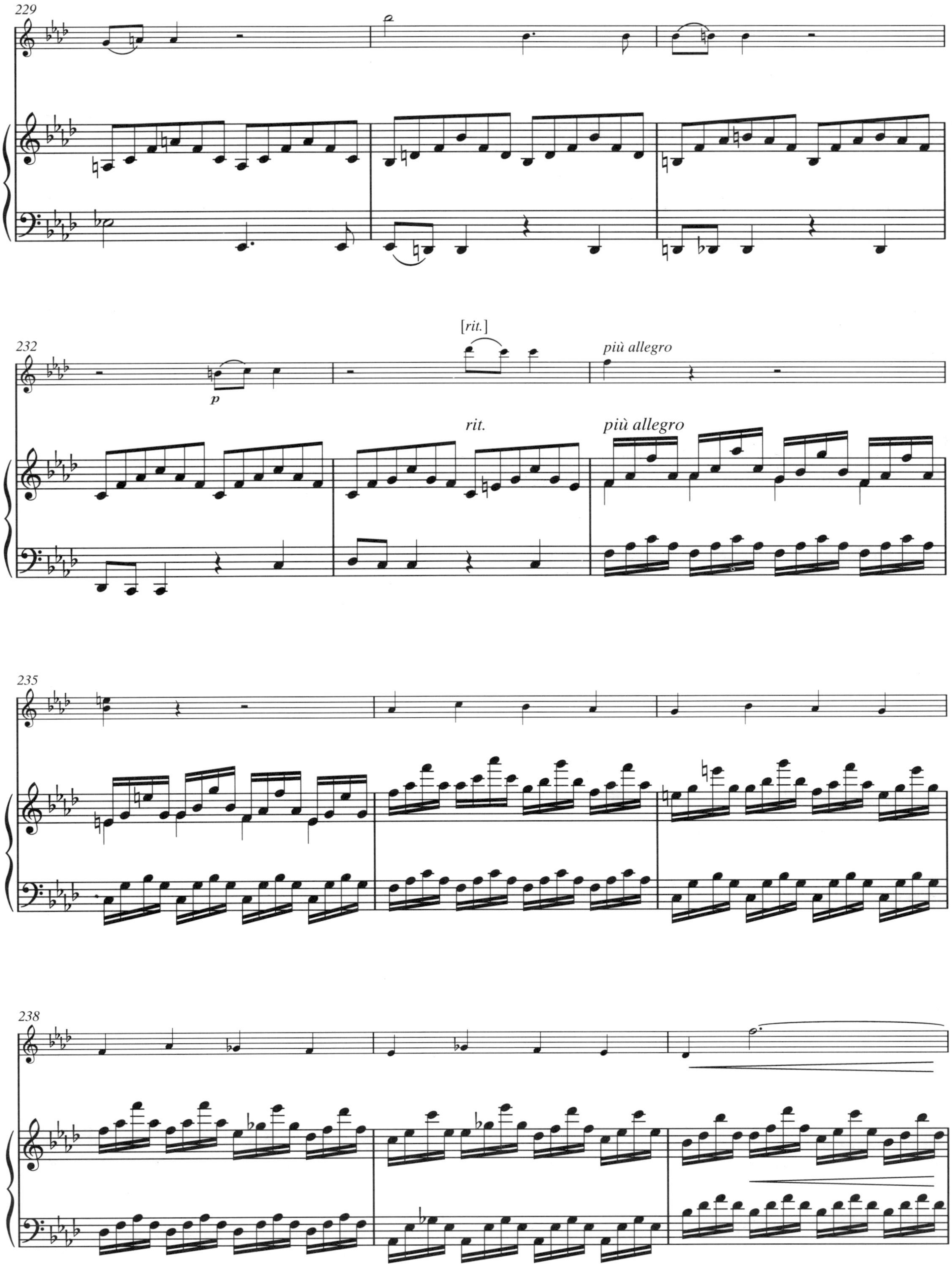
229
232
[rit.]
p
rit.
più allegro
più allegro
235
238

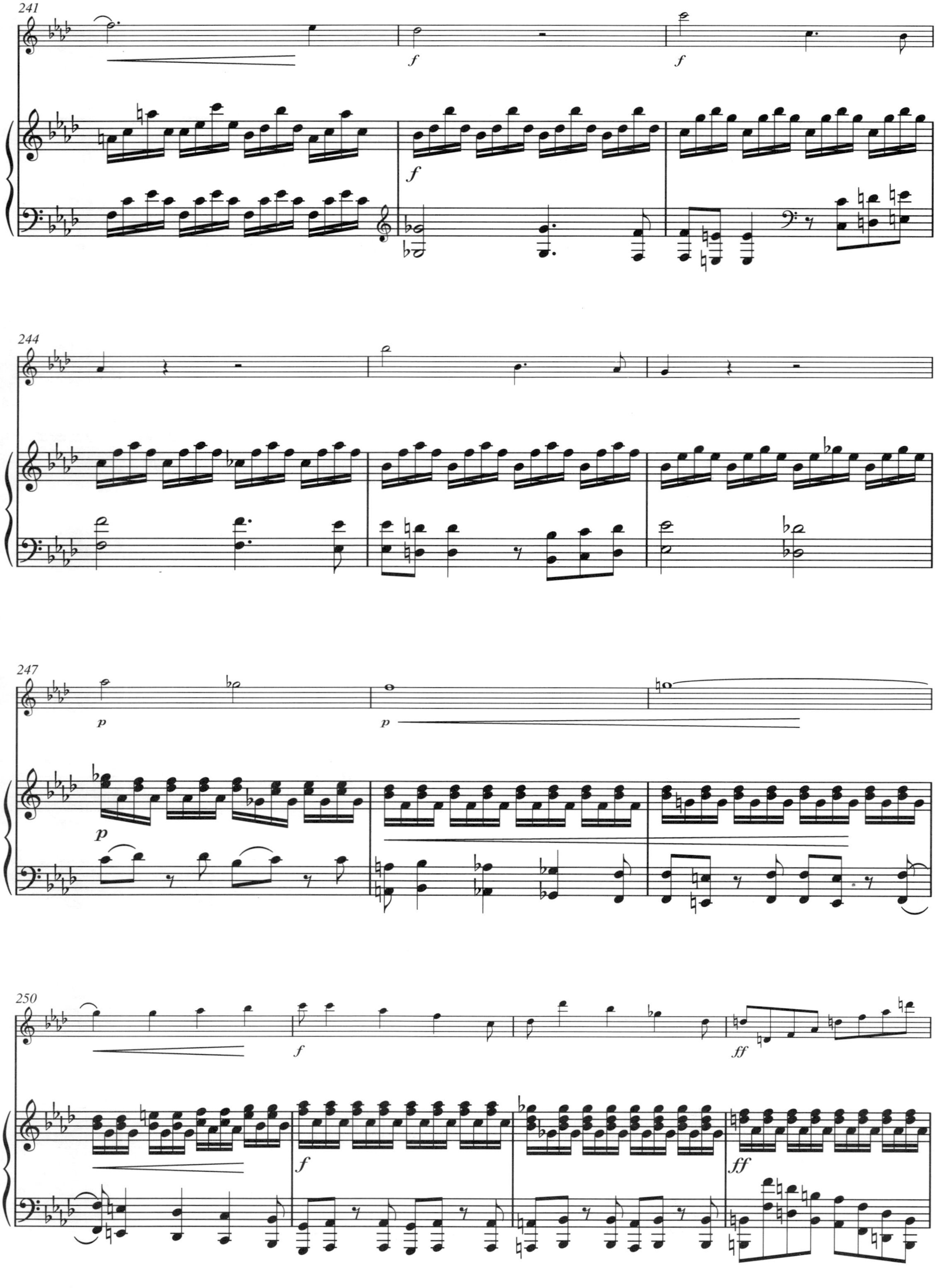
241
f
f
f
244
247
p
p
p
250
f
f
ff
ff

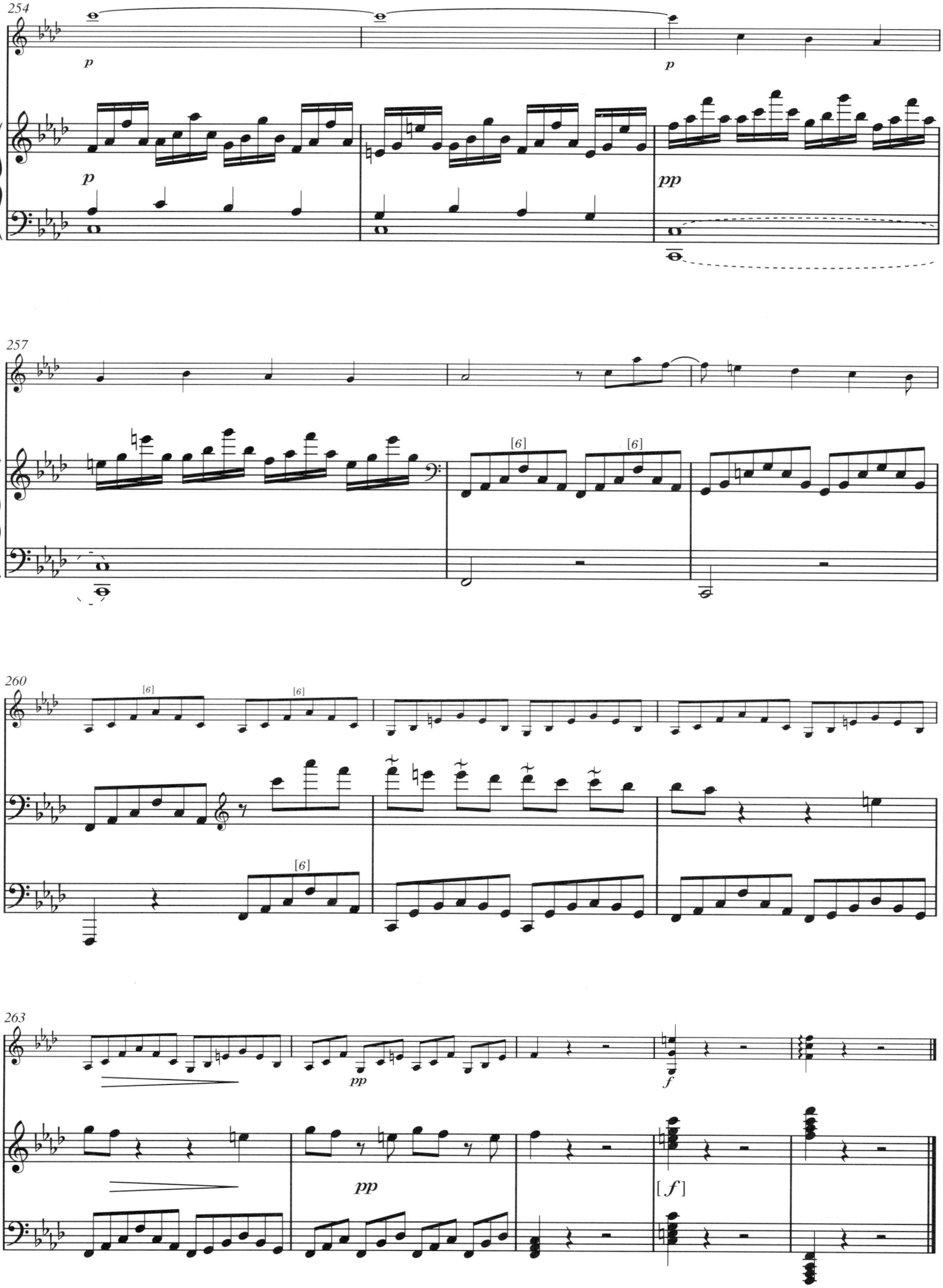
254
p
p
p
pp
257
[6]
[6]
260
[6]
[6]
[6]
263
pp
pp
f
[f]

Adagio
Adagio
[3]
p
f
sfz
p
6
p
9
p
sfz
sfz
ff
[simile]
sfz
p
sfz
sfz
sfz
12
p

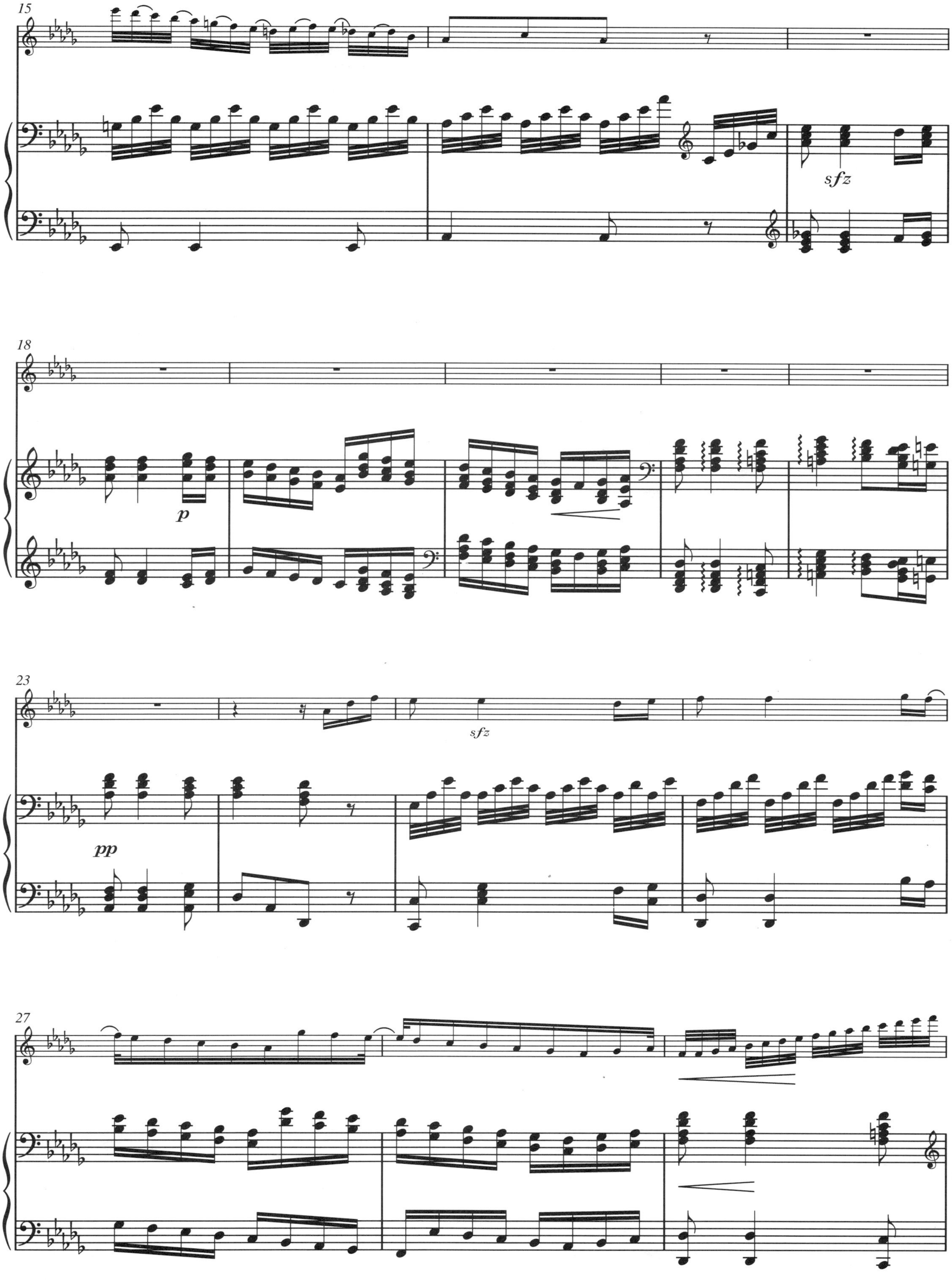
15
sfz
18
p
23
pp
sfz
27

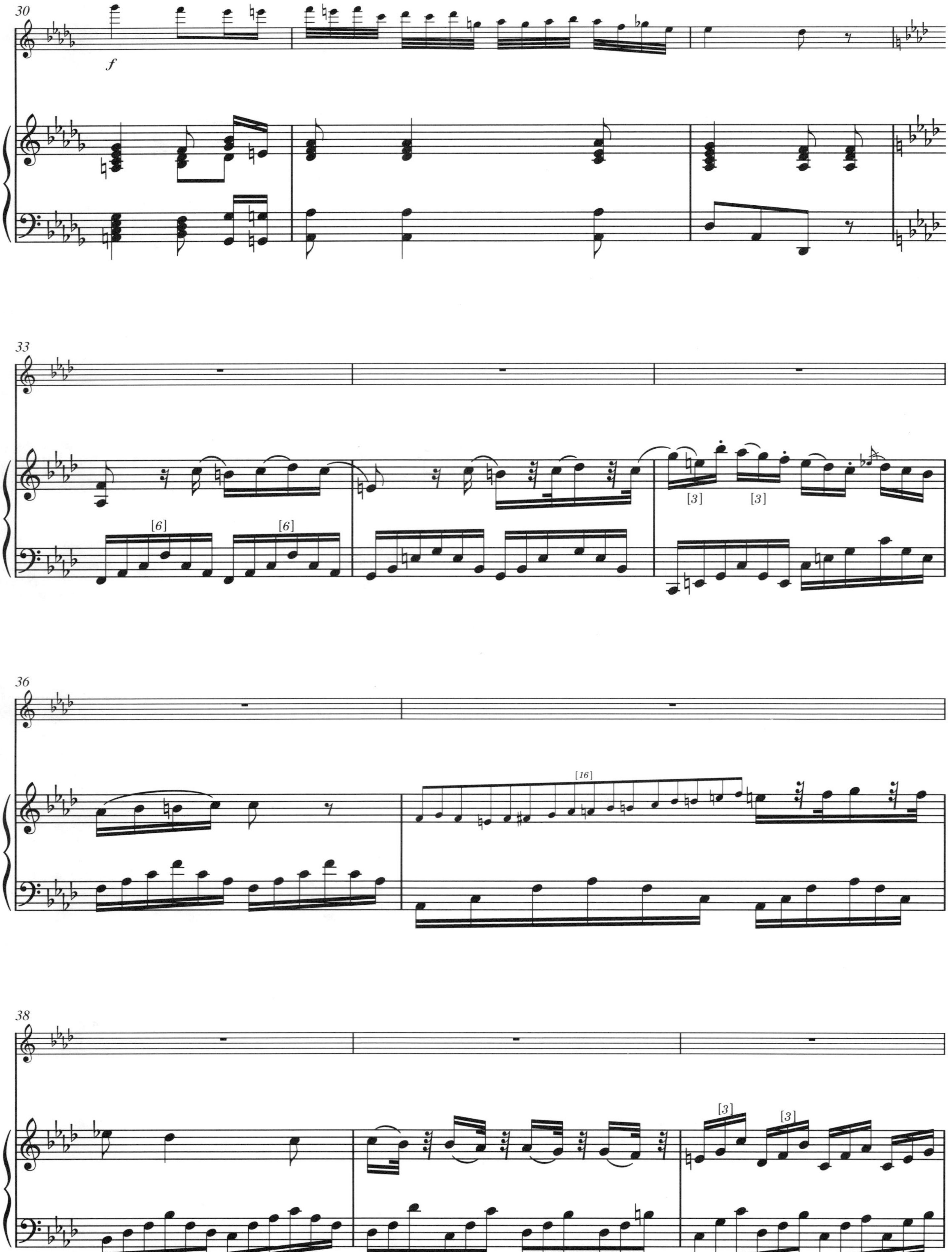
30
f
33
[6]
[6]
[3]
[3]
36
[16]
38
[3]
[3]

65

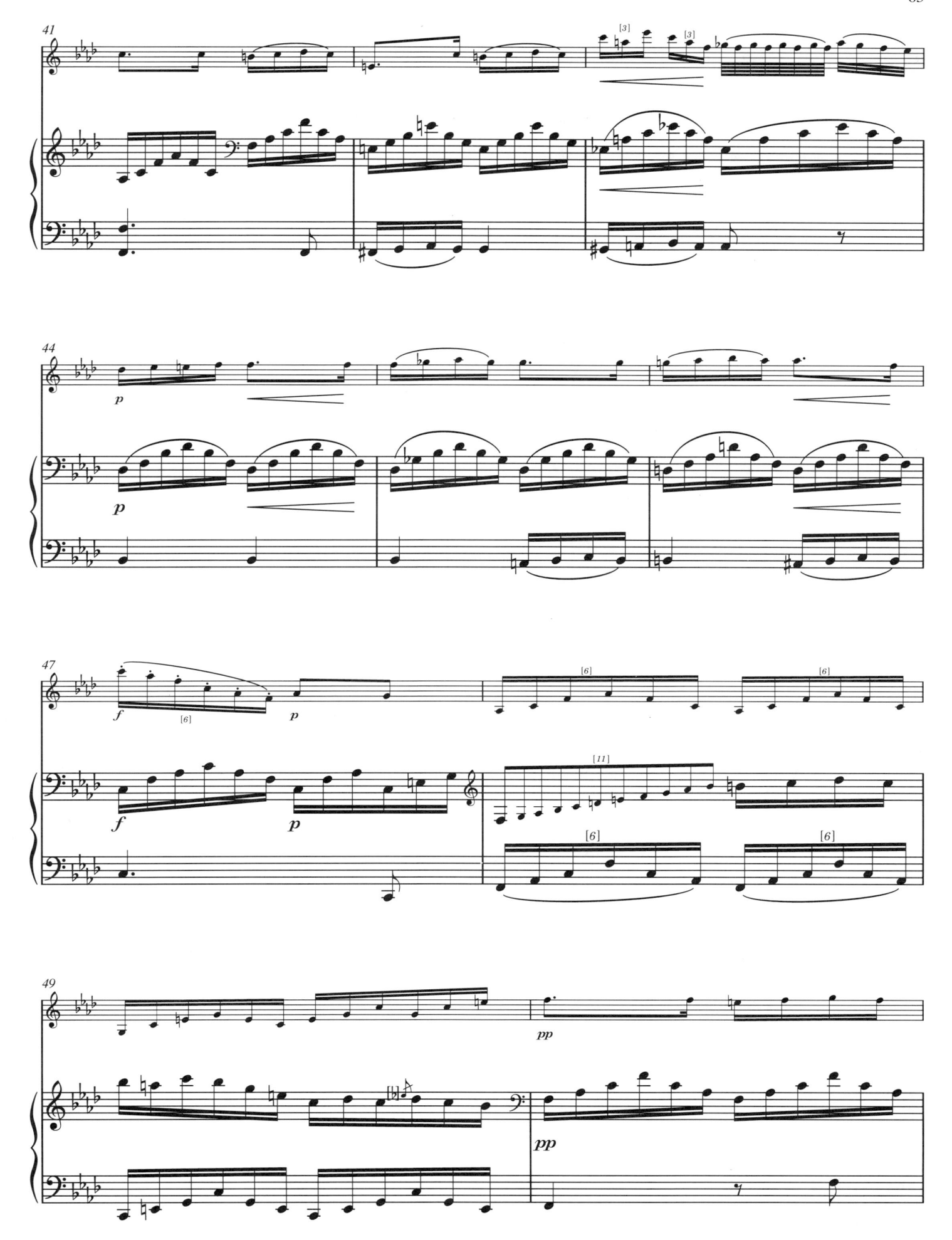

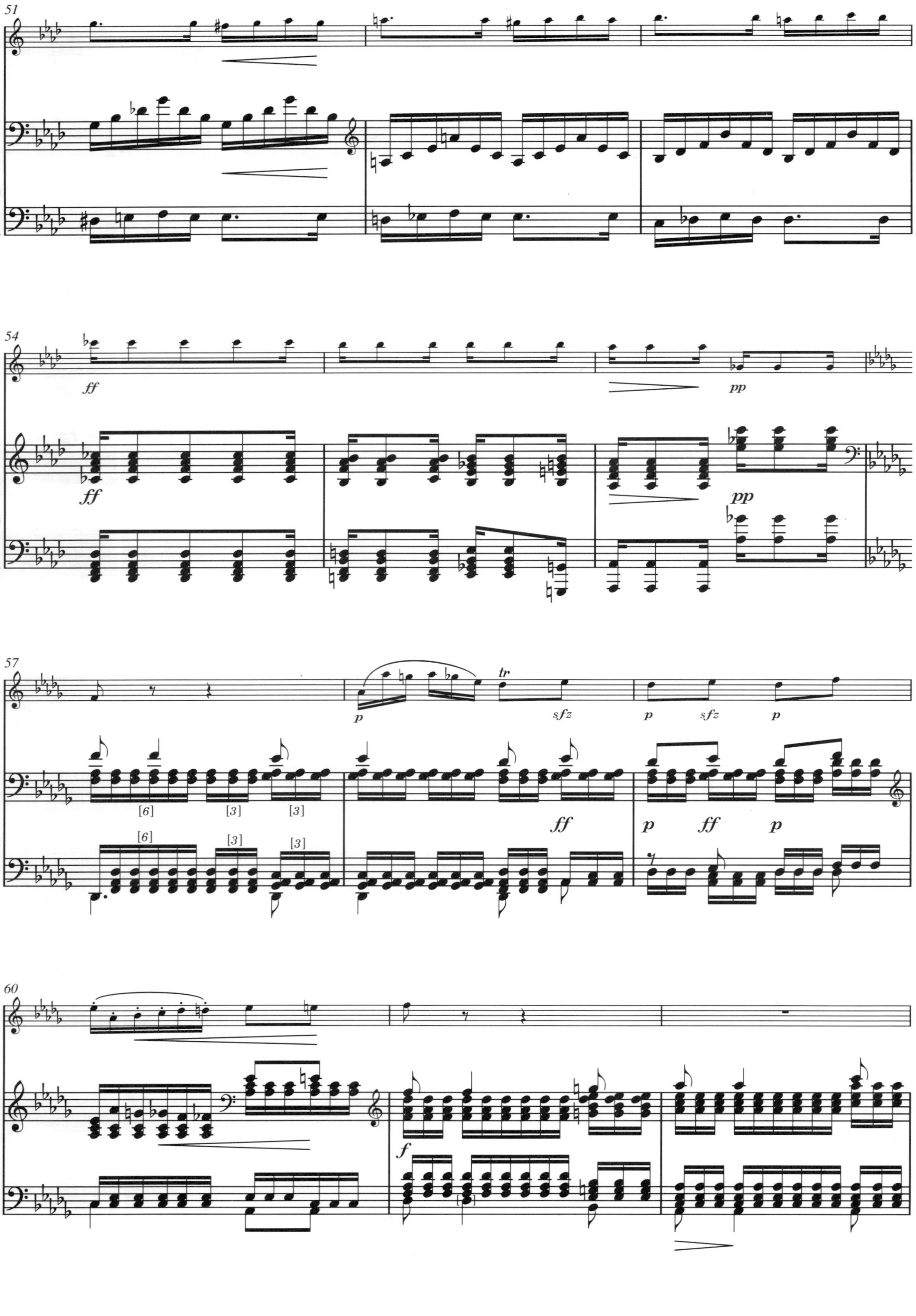
51
54
ff
pp
57
p
sfz
tr
[6]
[3]
60
f

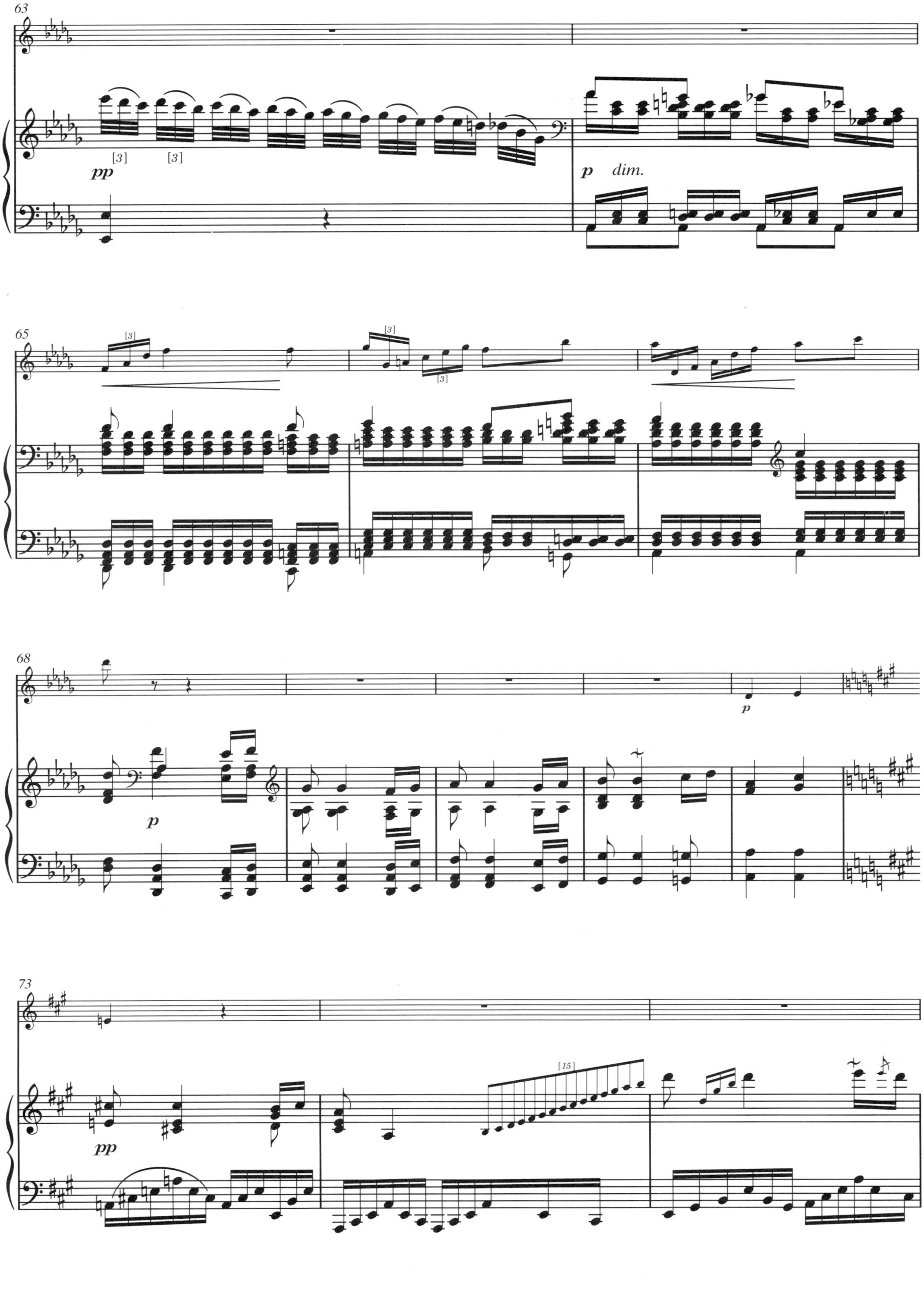
63
[3]
[3]
pp
p
dim.
65
[3]
[3]
[3]
68
p
p
73
pp
[15]

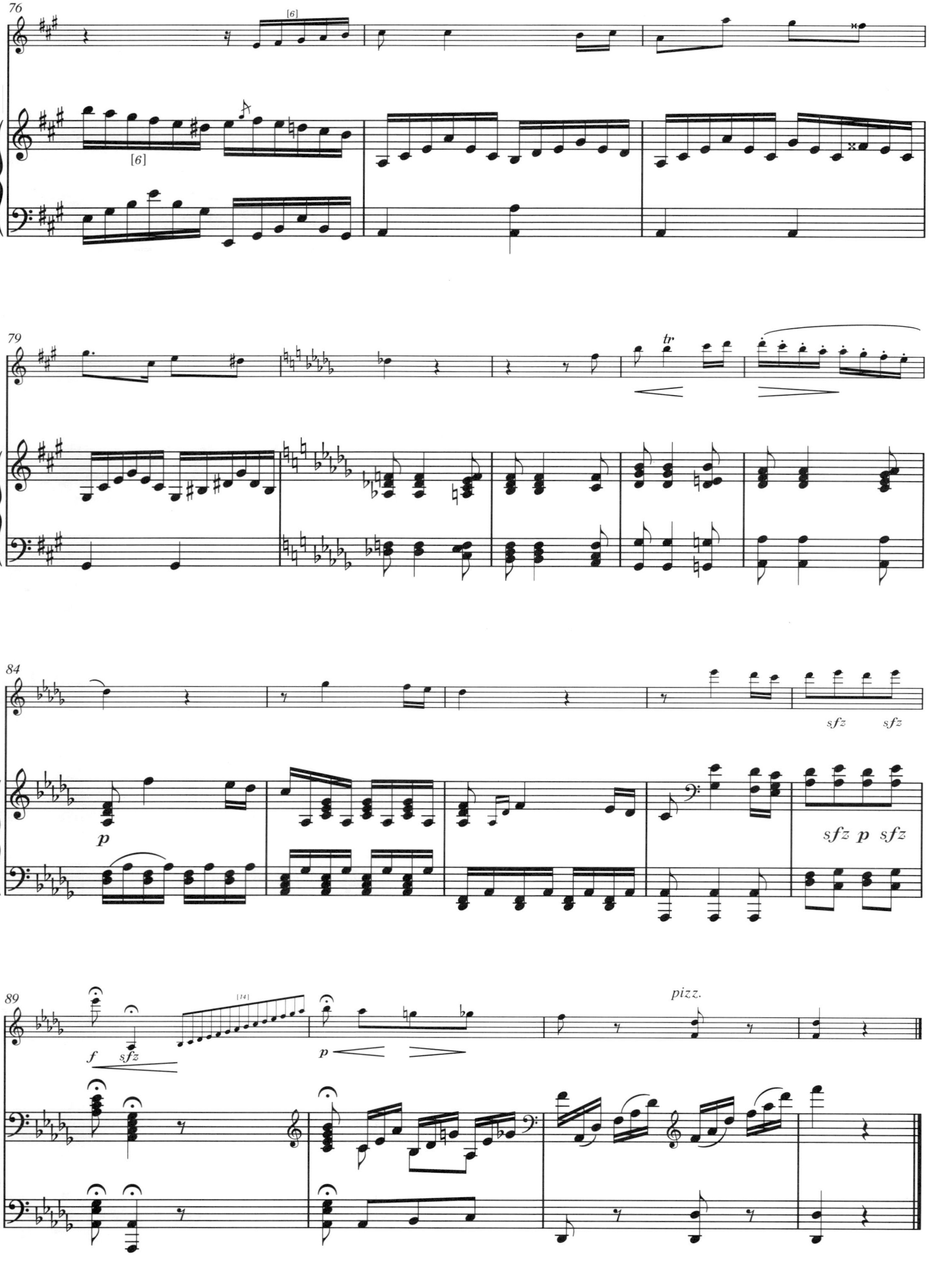
76
[6]
[6]
79
tr
84
p
sfz
sfz
sfz p sfz
89
[14]
f
sfz
p
pizz.

Menuetto
Allegro molto

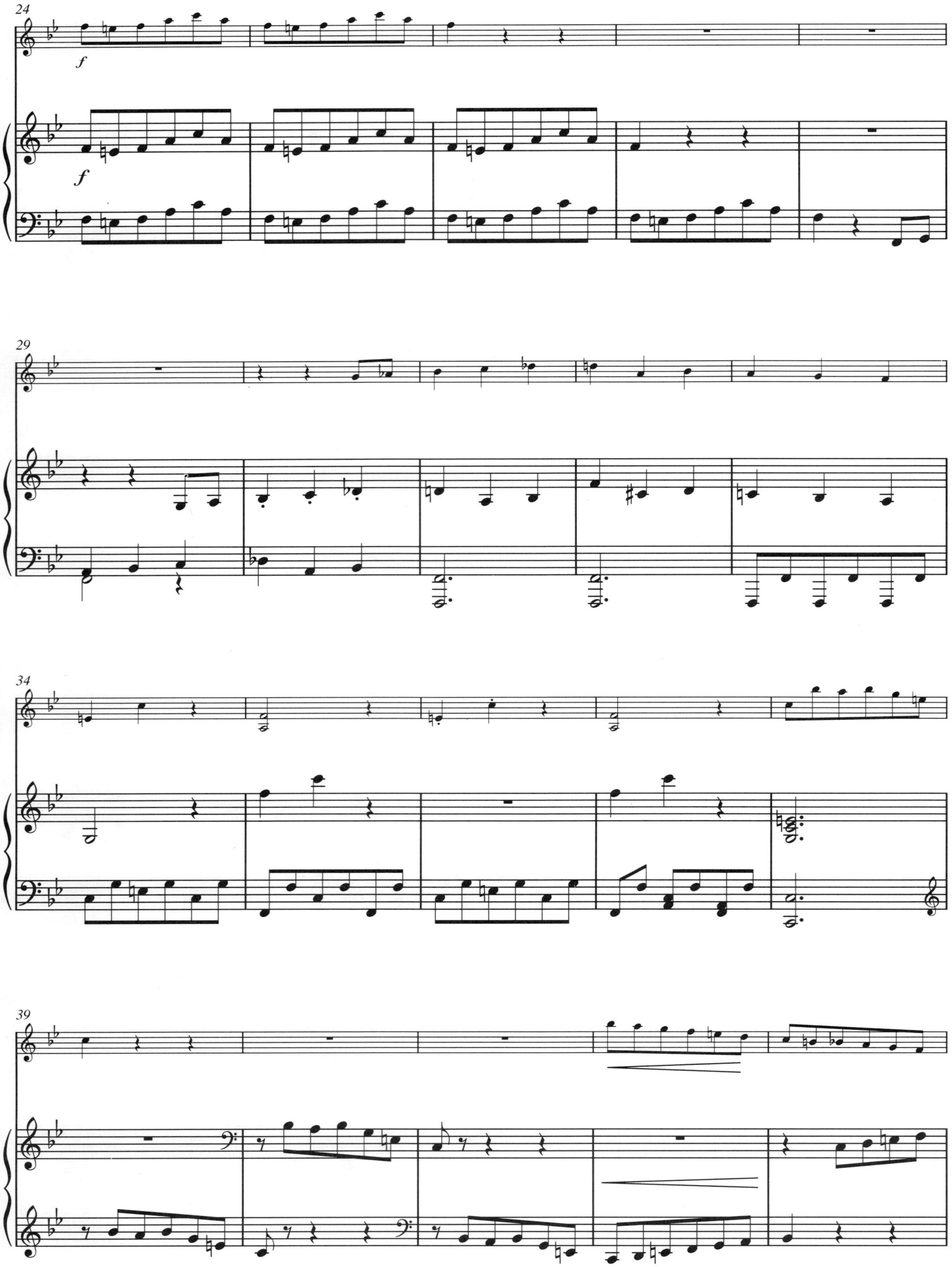
24
f
f
29
34
39

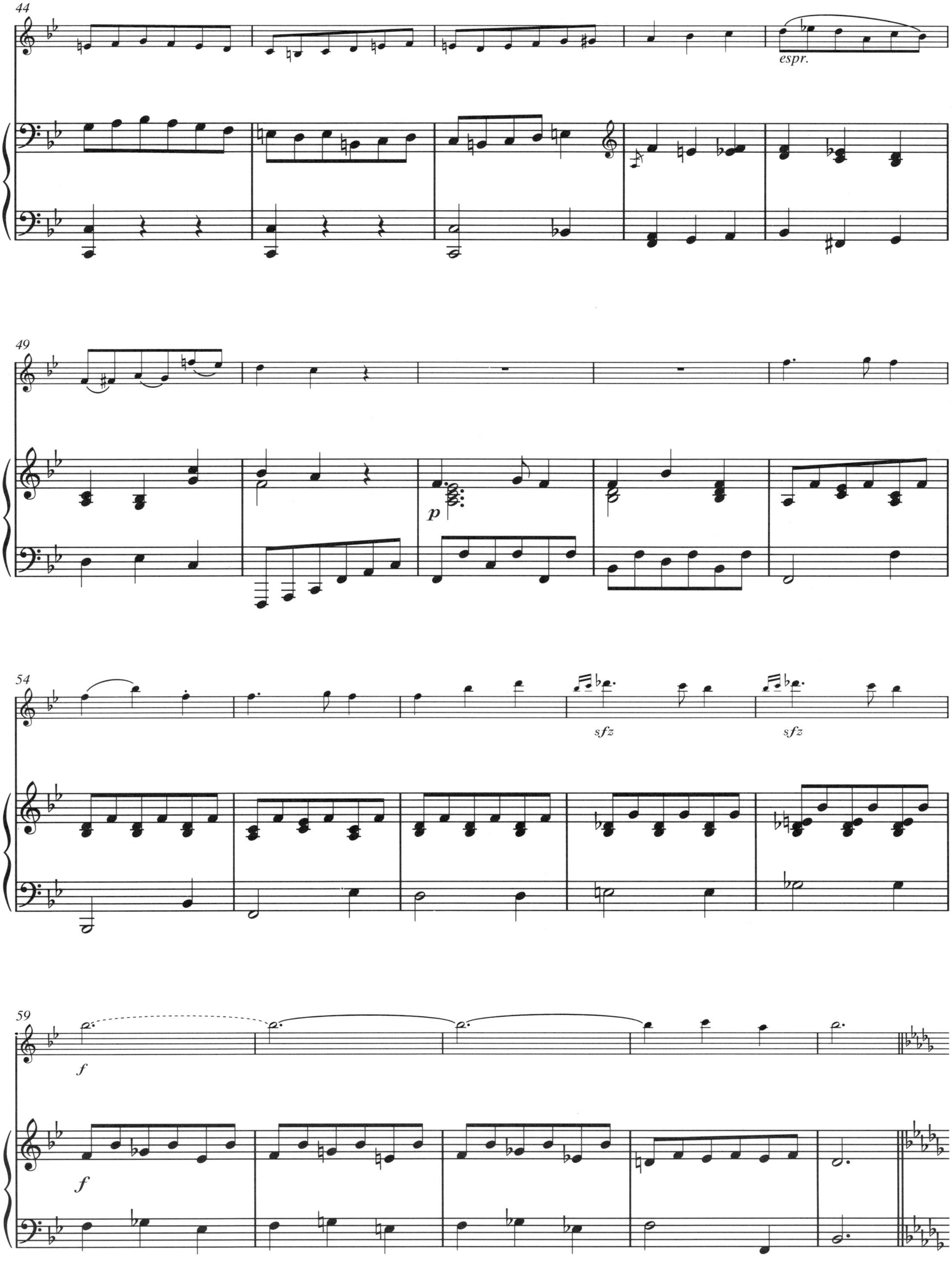
44
espr.
49
p
54
sfz
sfz
59
f
f

Trio I

Menuetto
Allegro molto

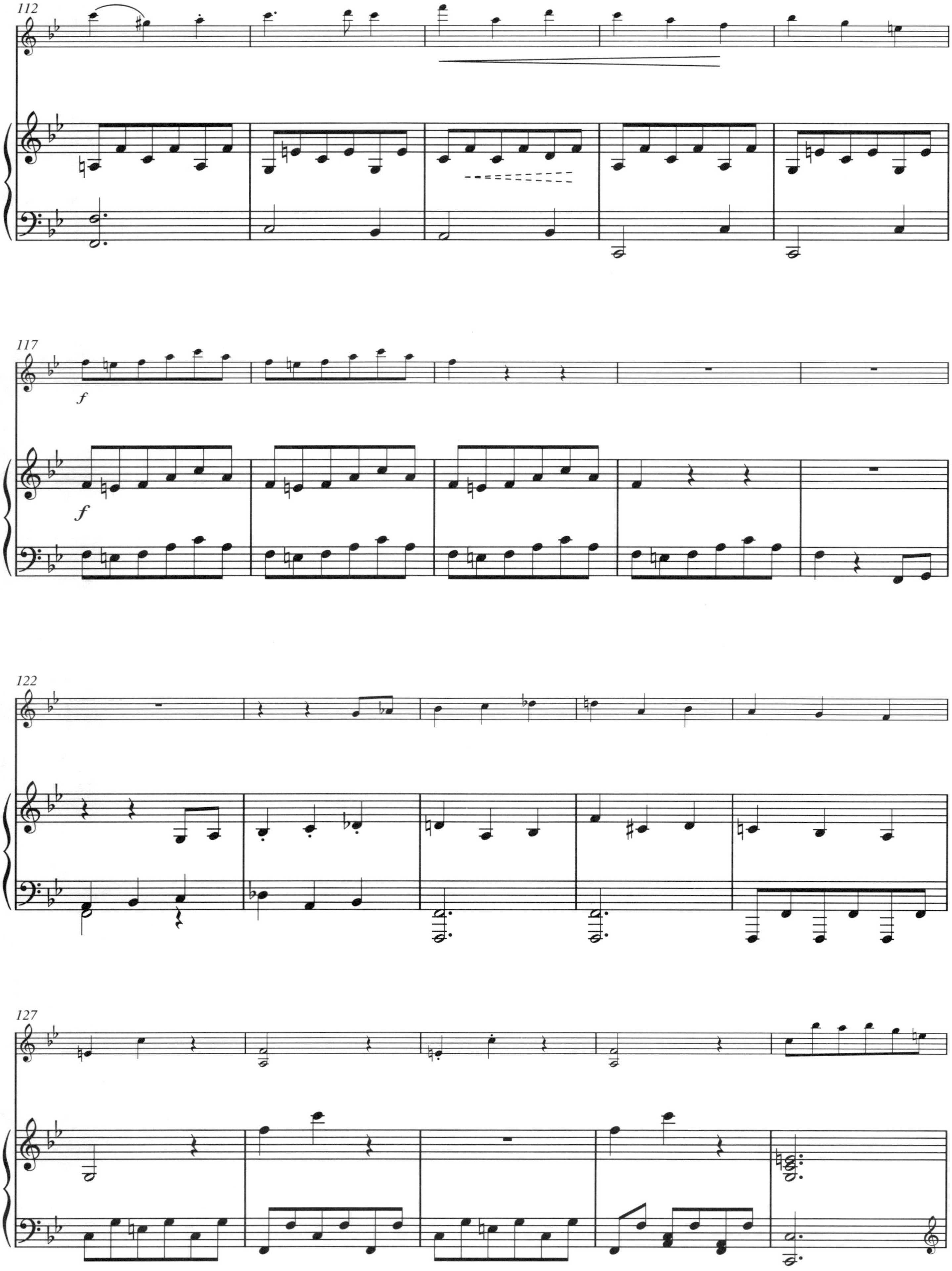
112
117
f
f
122
127

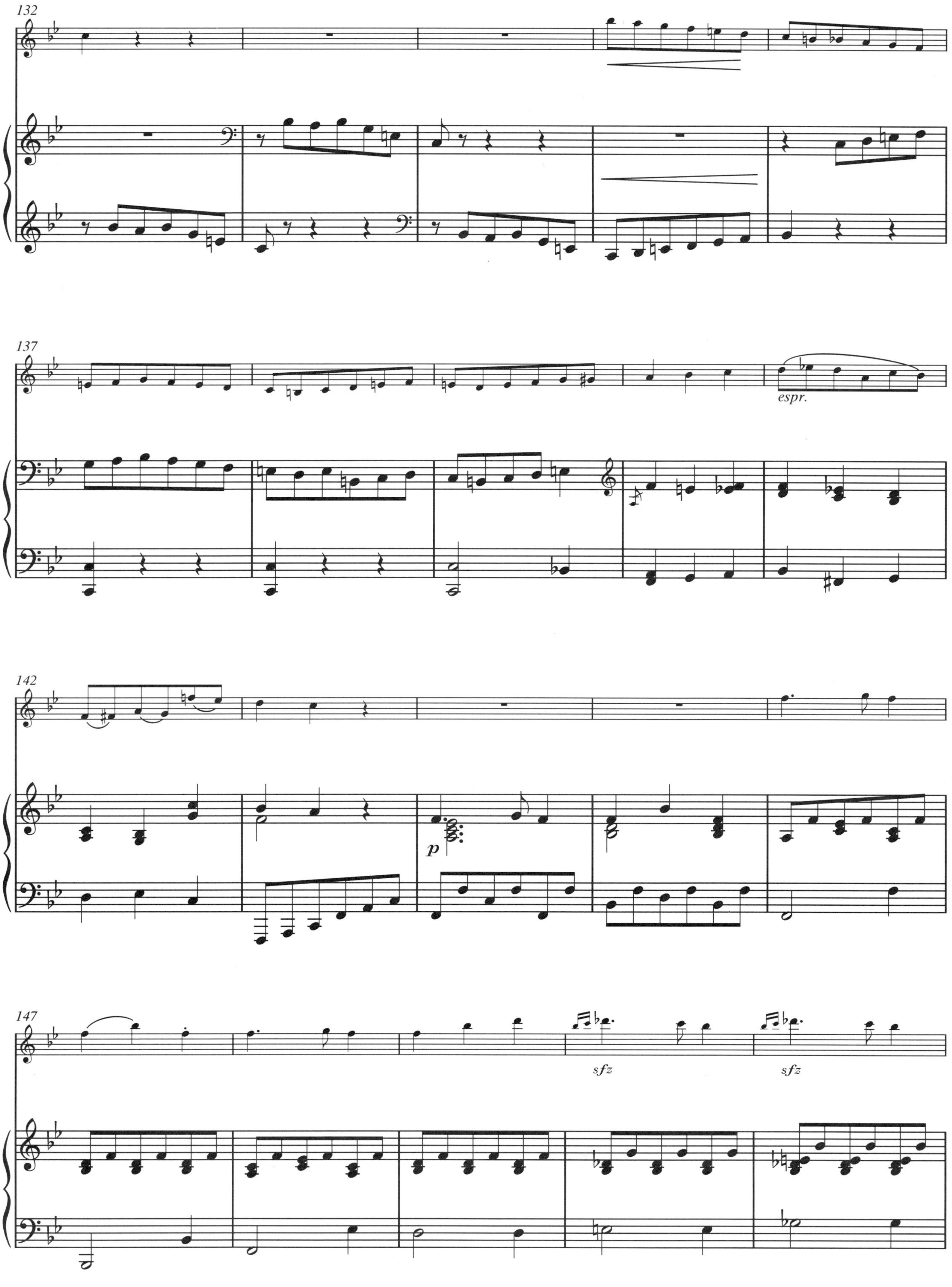
132
137
espr.
142
p
147
sfz
sfz

76

173
sfz
178
f
rit.
a tempo
f
sf
rit.
a tempo
f
183
188
1.
2.
ritard.
a piacere
1.
2.
ritard.
p

Menuetto
Allegro molto

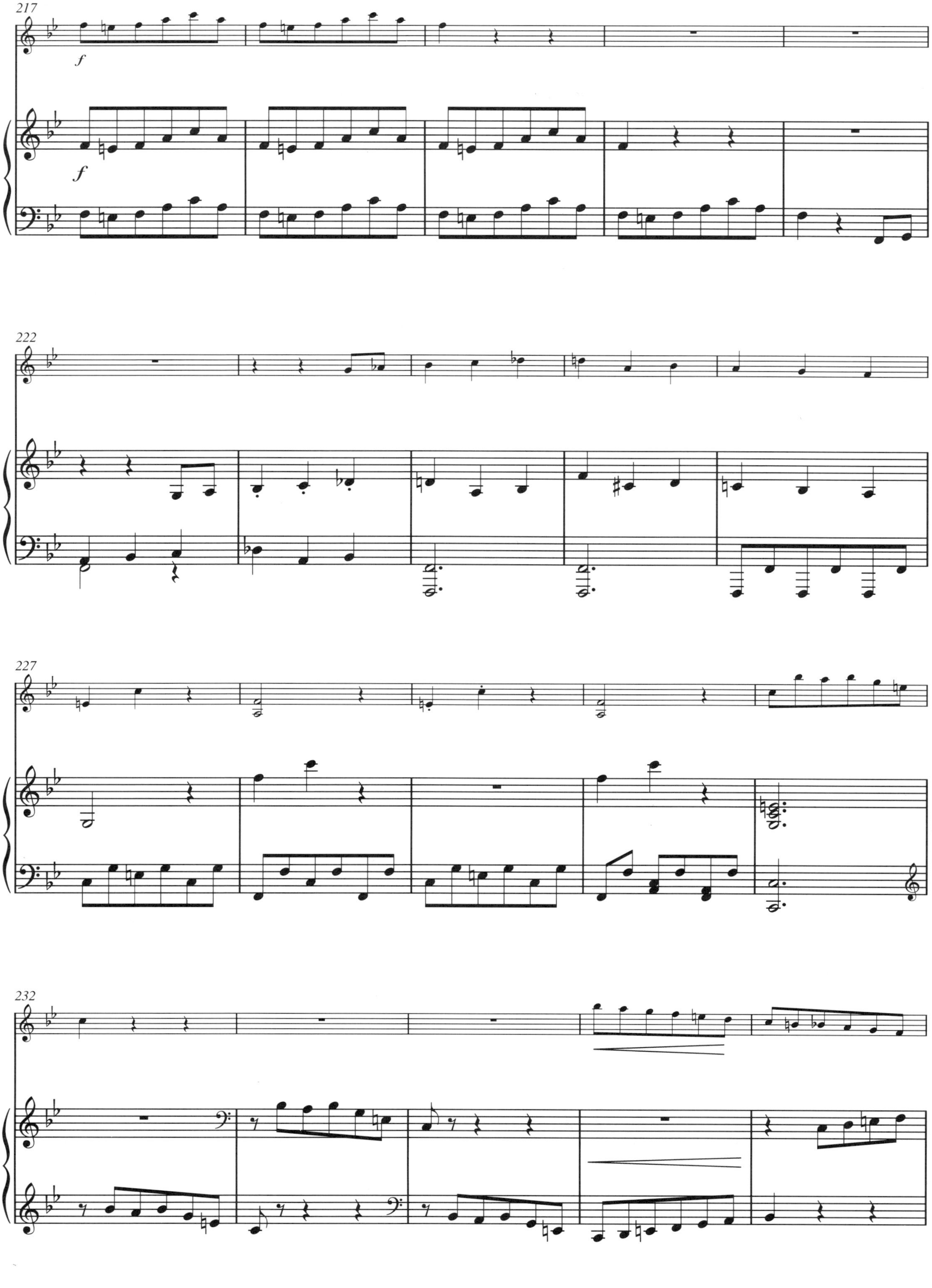
217
f
f
222
227
232

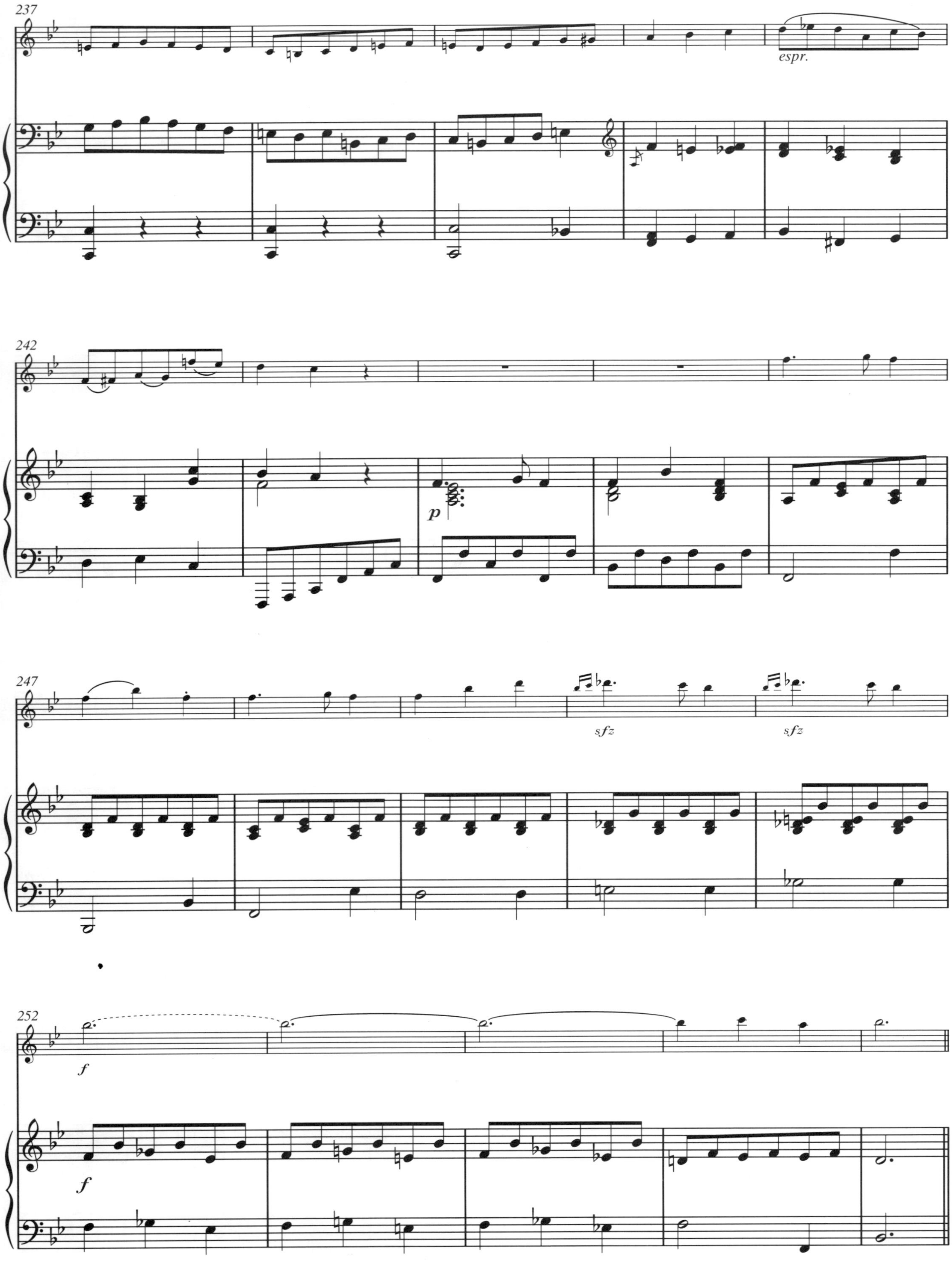
237
espr.
242
p
247
sfz
sfz
252
f
f

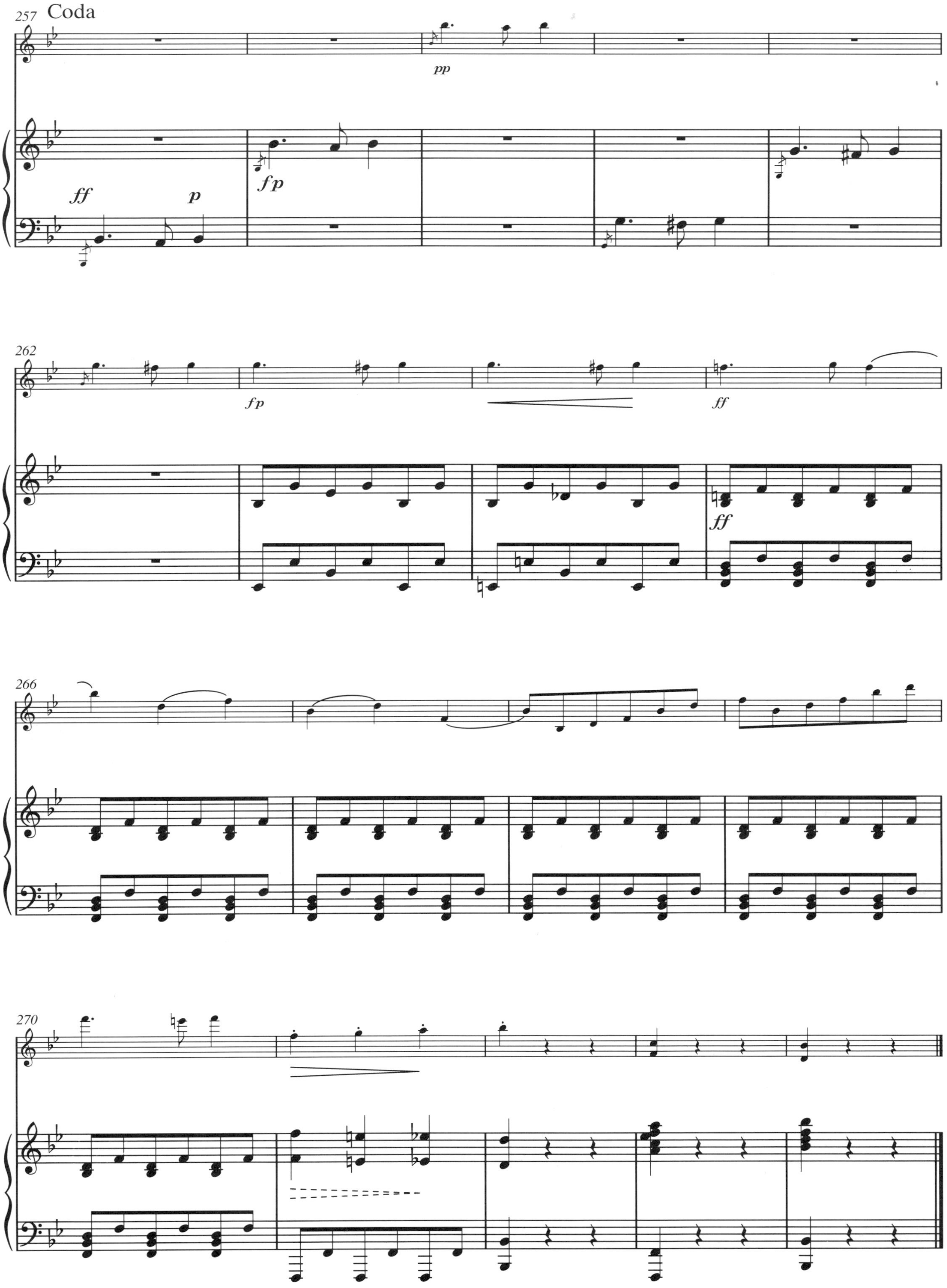
257
Coda
pp
ff
p
fp
262
fp
ff
ff
266
270

Allegro assai quasi presto
Allegro assai quasi presto
p
6
sfz p
sfz p
12
pp
[p]
18
f
f
a piacere

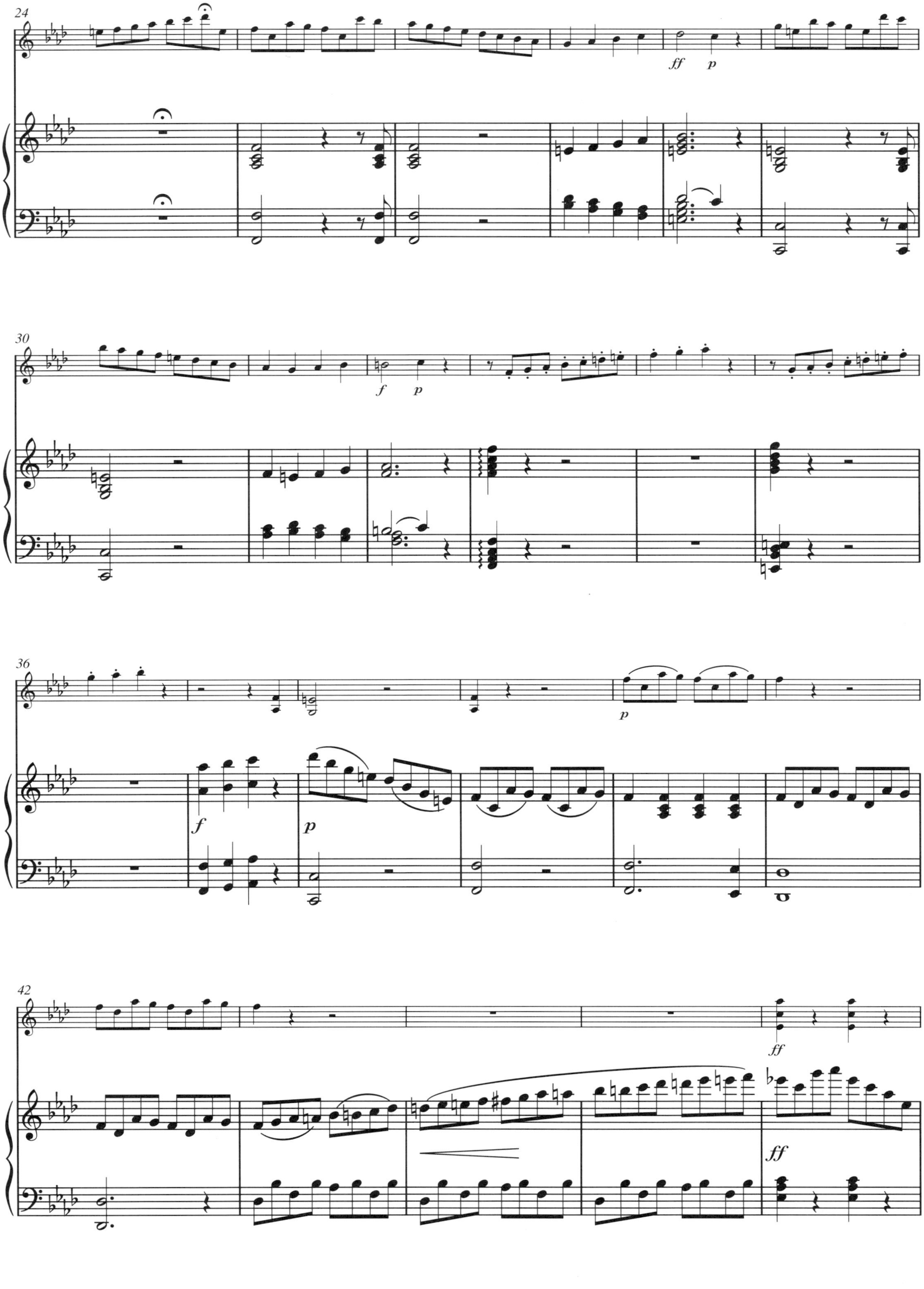
24
ff p
30
f p
36
f
p
p
42
ff
ff

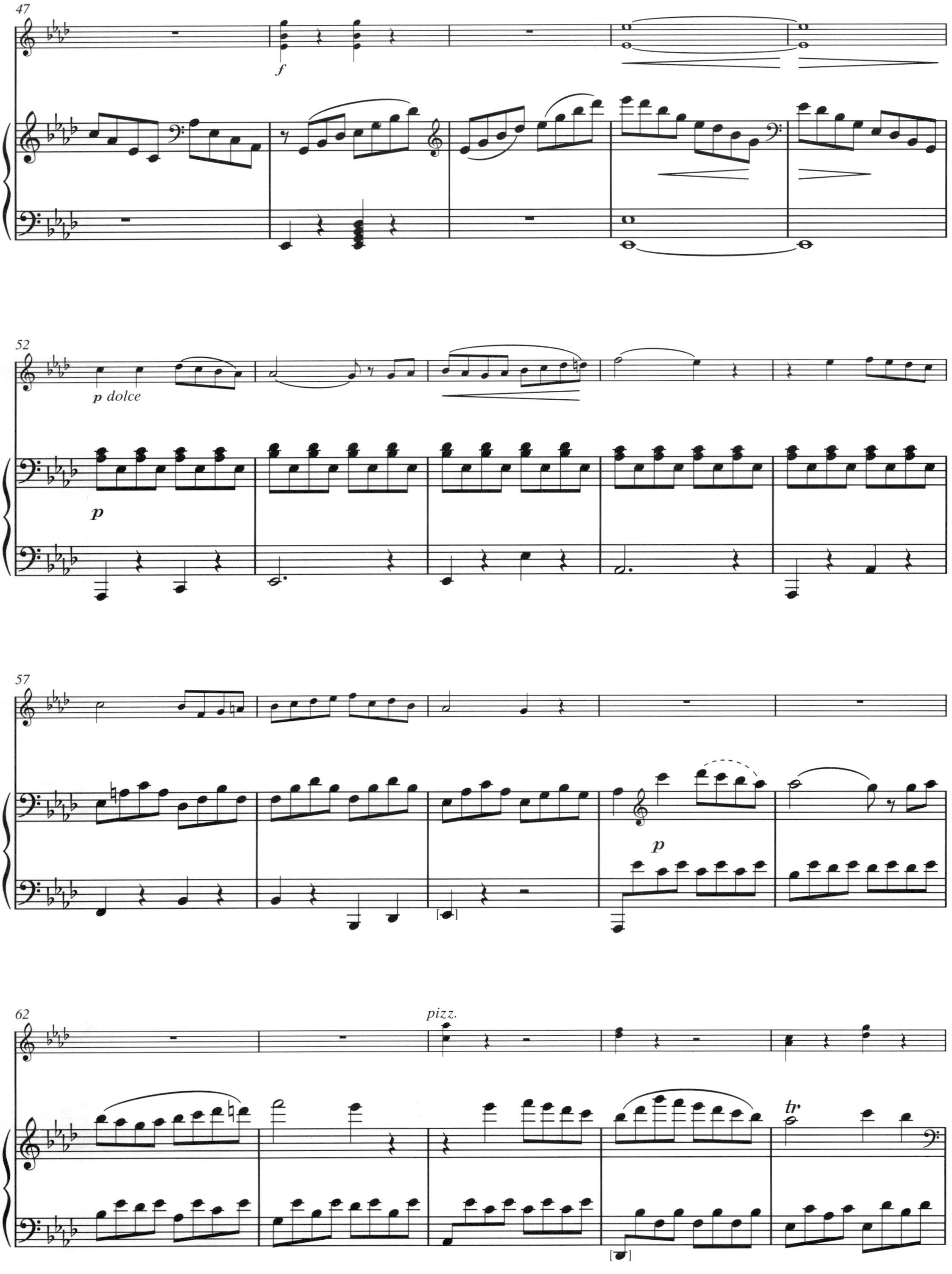
47
f
52
p dolce
p
57
p
62
pizz.
tr

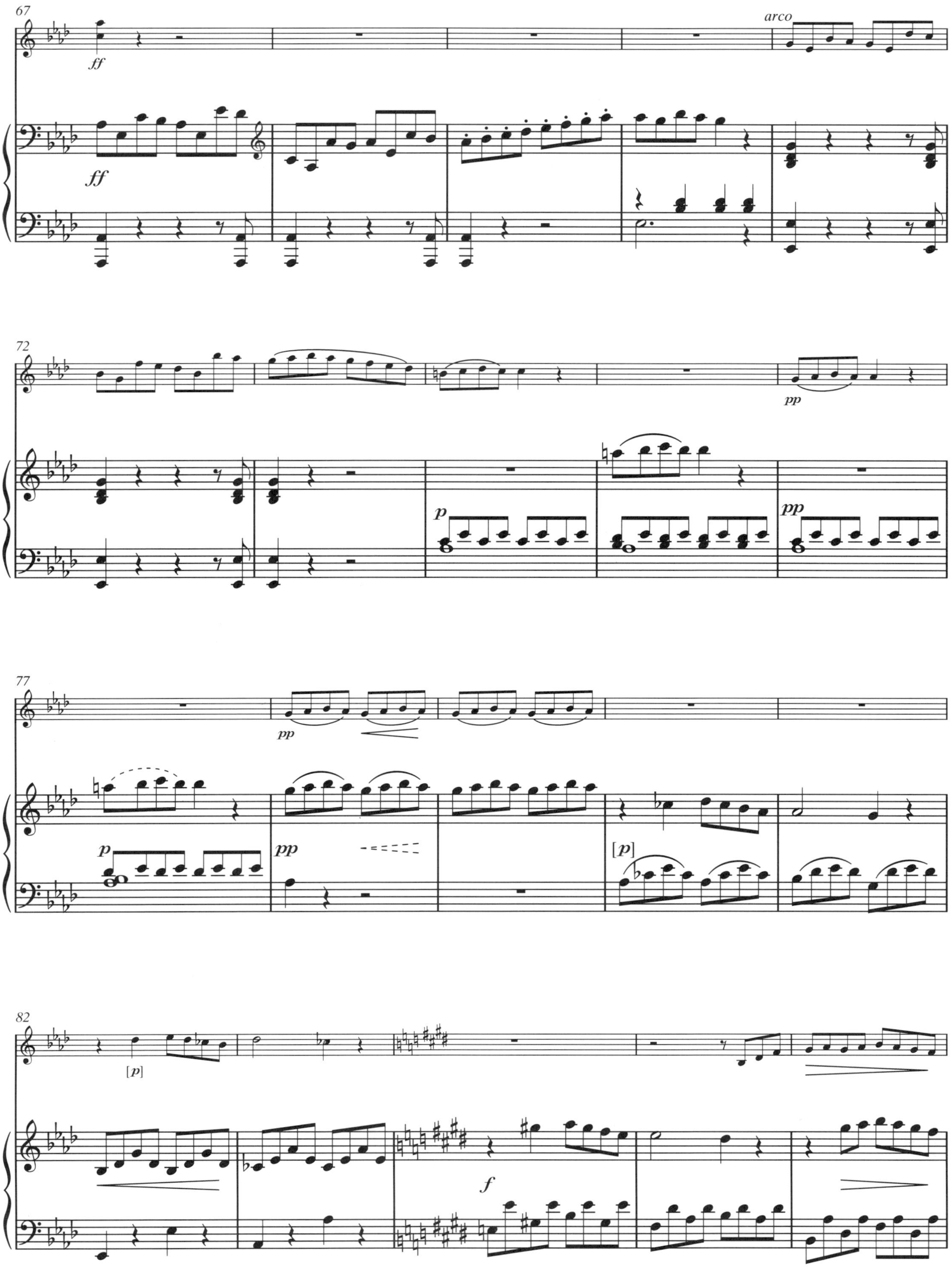
67
ff
ff
arco
72
pp
p
pp
77
pp
p
pp
[p]
82
[p]
f

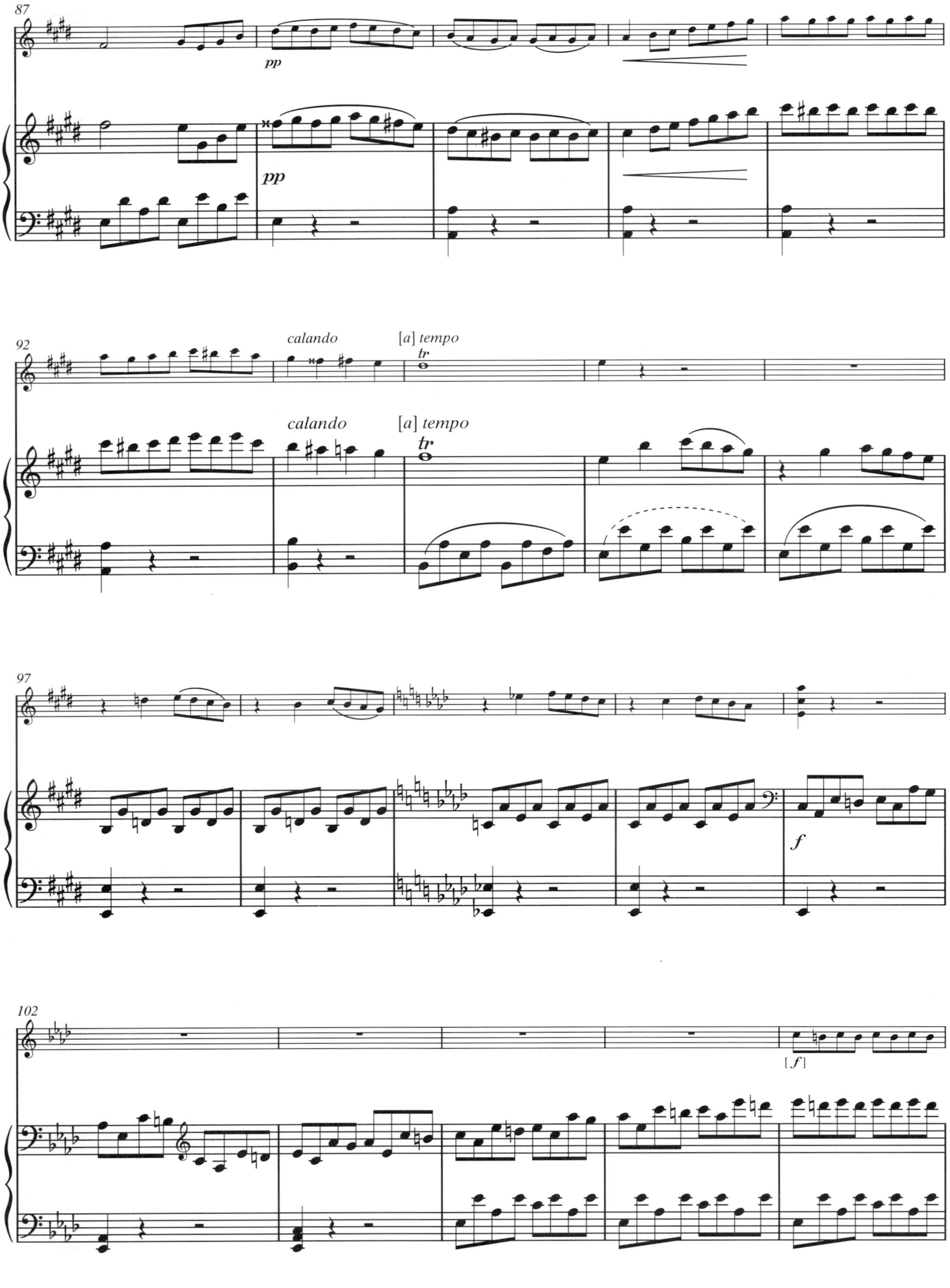
87
pp
pp
92
calando
[a] tempo
tr
calando
[a] tempo
tr
97
f
102
[f]

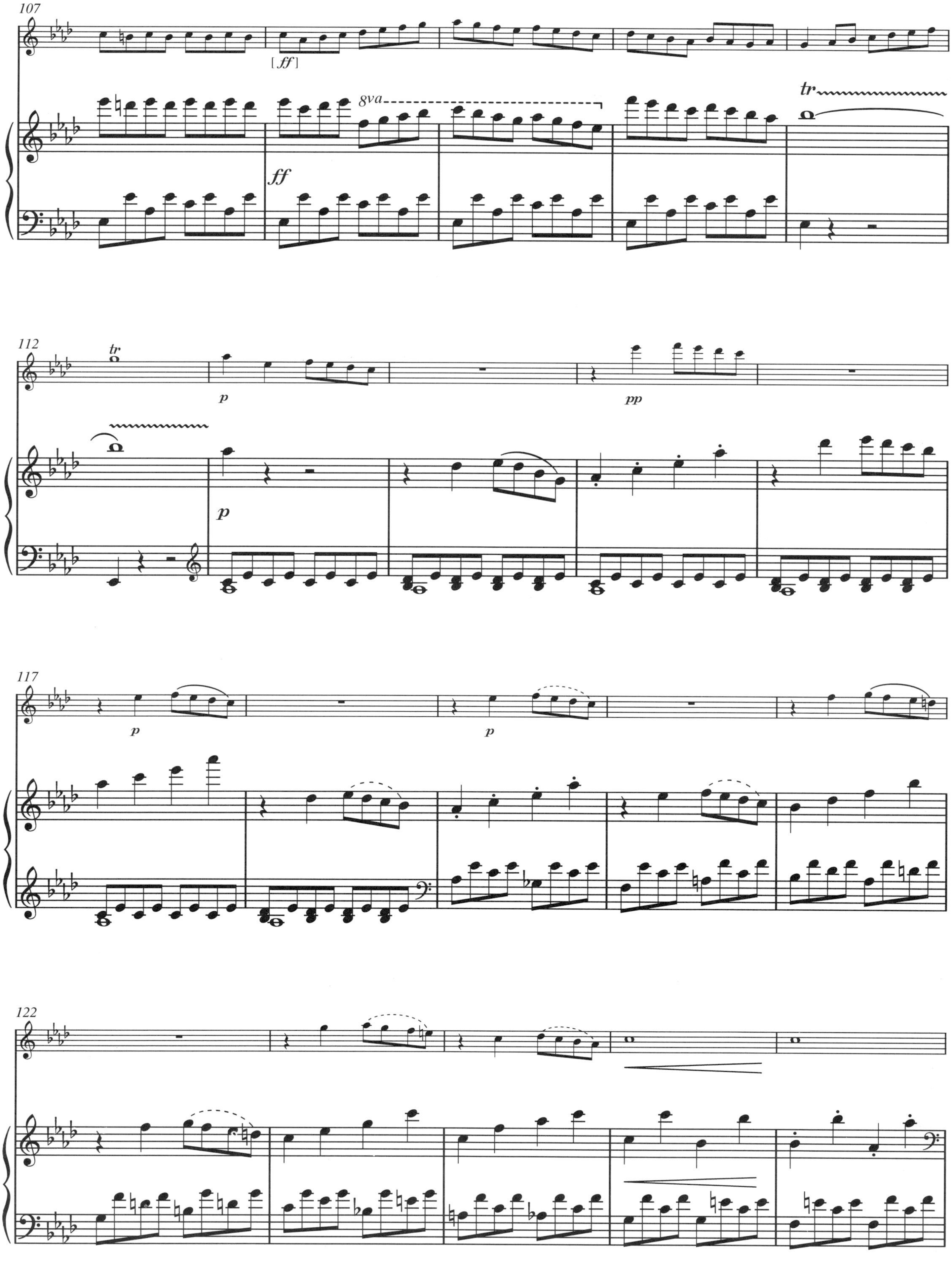
107
[ff]
8va
ff
tr
112
tr
p
pp
p
117
p
p
122

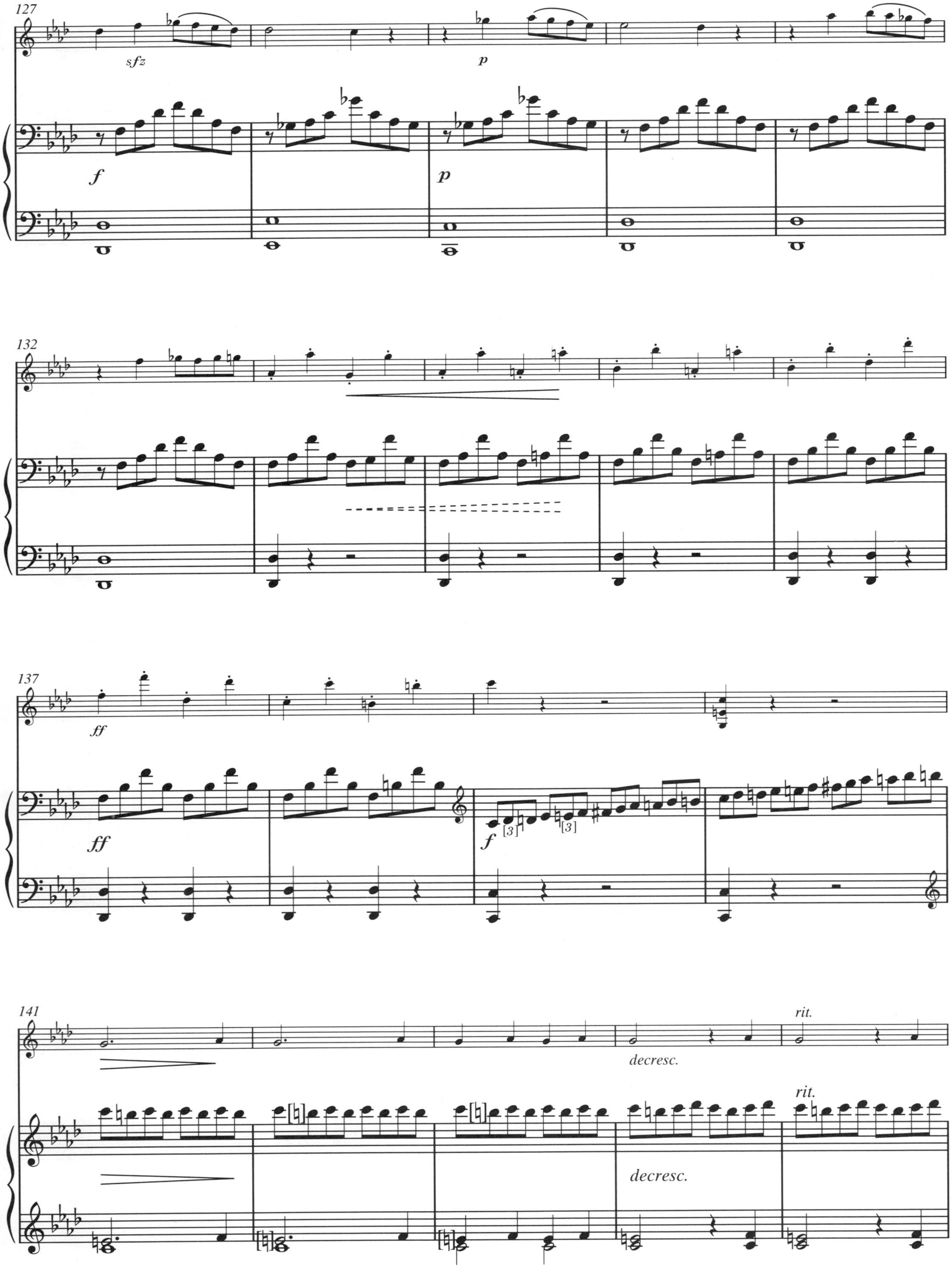
127
sfz
p
f
p
132
137
ff
ff
f
[3]
[3]
141
rit.
decresc.
rit.
decresc.

146
pp
tr
a piacere
pp
153
presto
ff
158
a tempo
calando
a tempo
sfz
p
164
p
[f]
fp
f

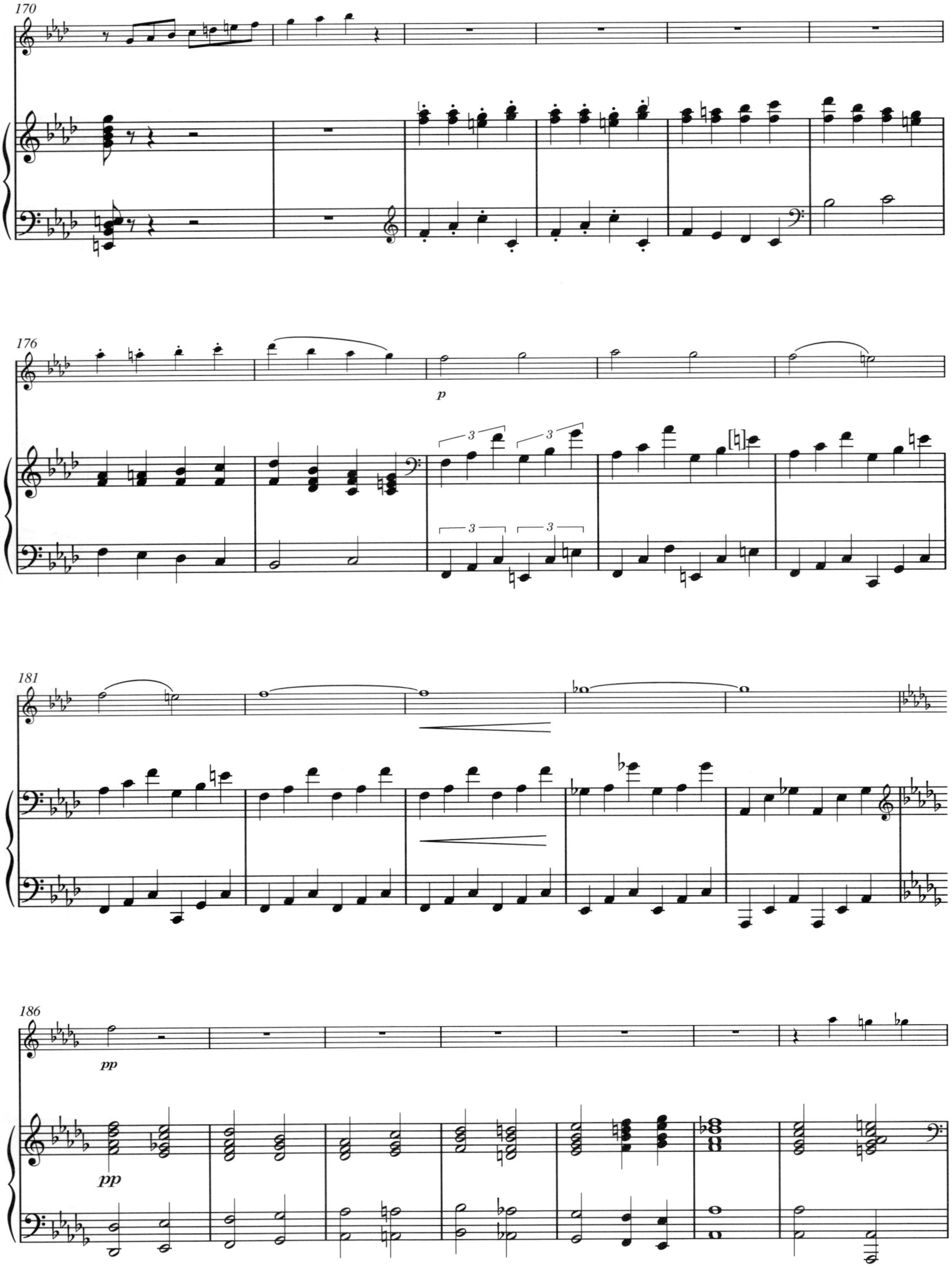
170
176
p
181
186
pp
pp

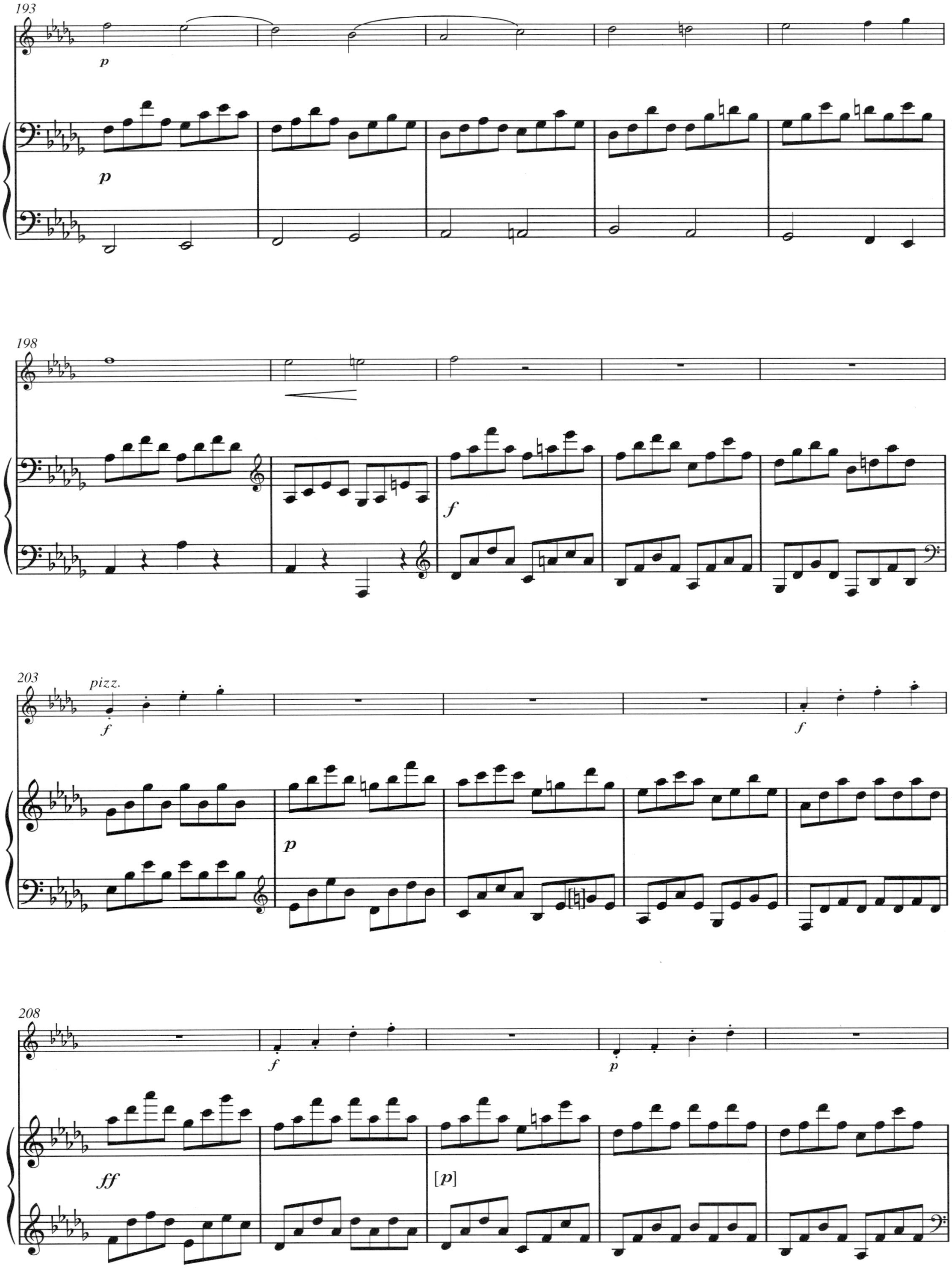
193
p
p
198
f
203
pizz.
f
p
f
208
f
p
ff
[p]

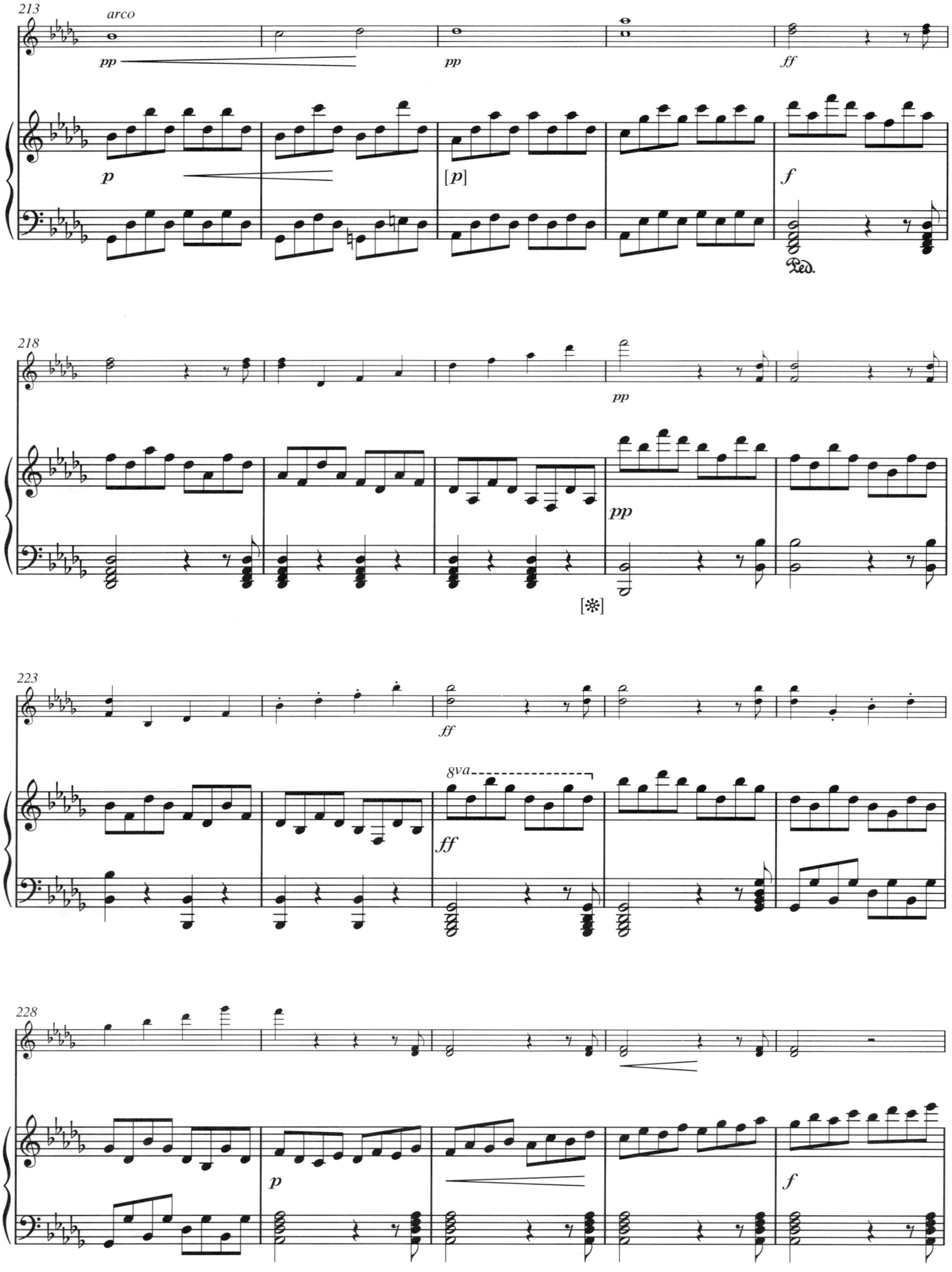
213
arco
pp
pp
ff
p
[p]
f
Ped.
218
pp
pp
[※]
223
ff
8va
ff
228
p
f

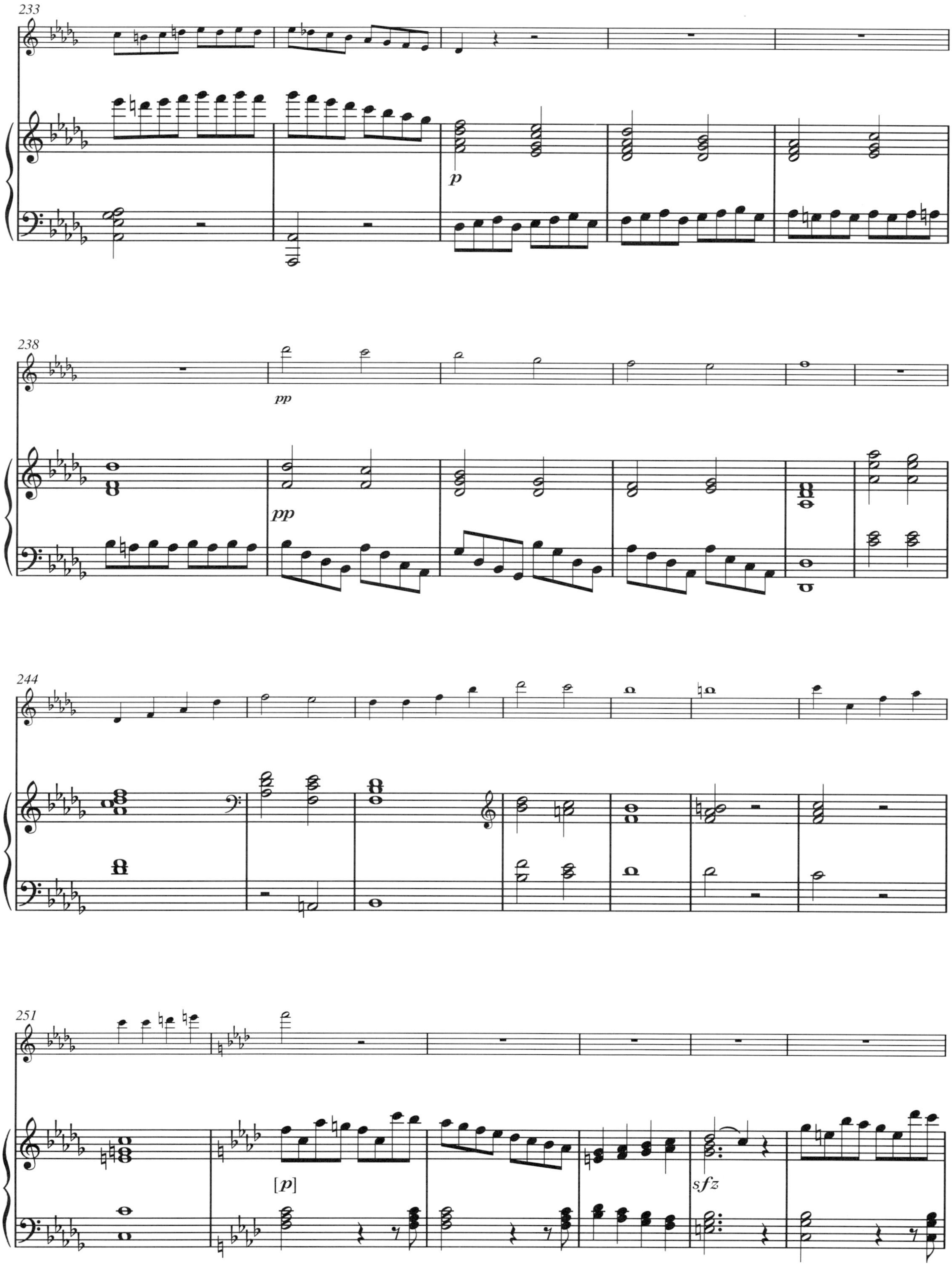
233
p
238
pp
pp
244
251
[p]
sfz

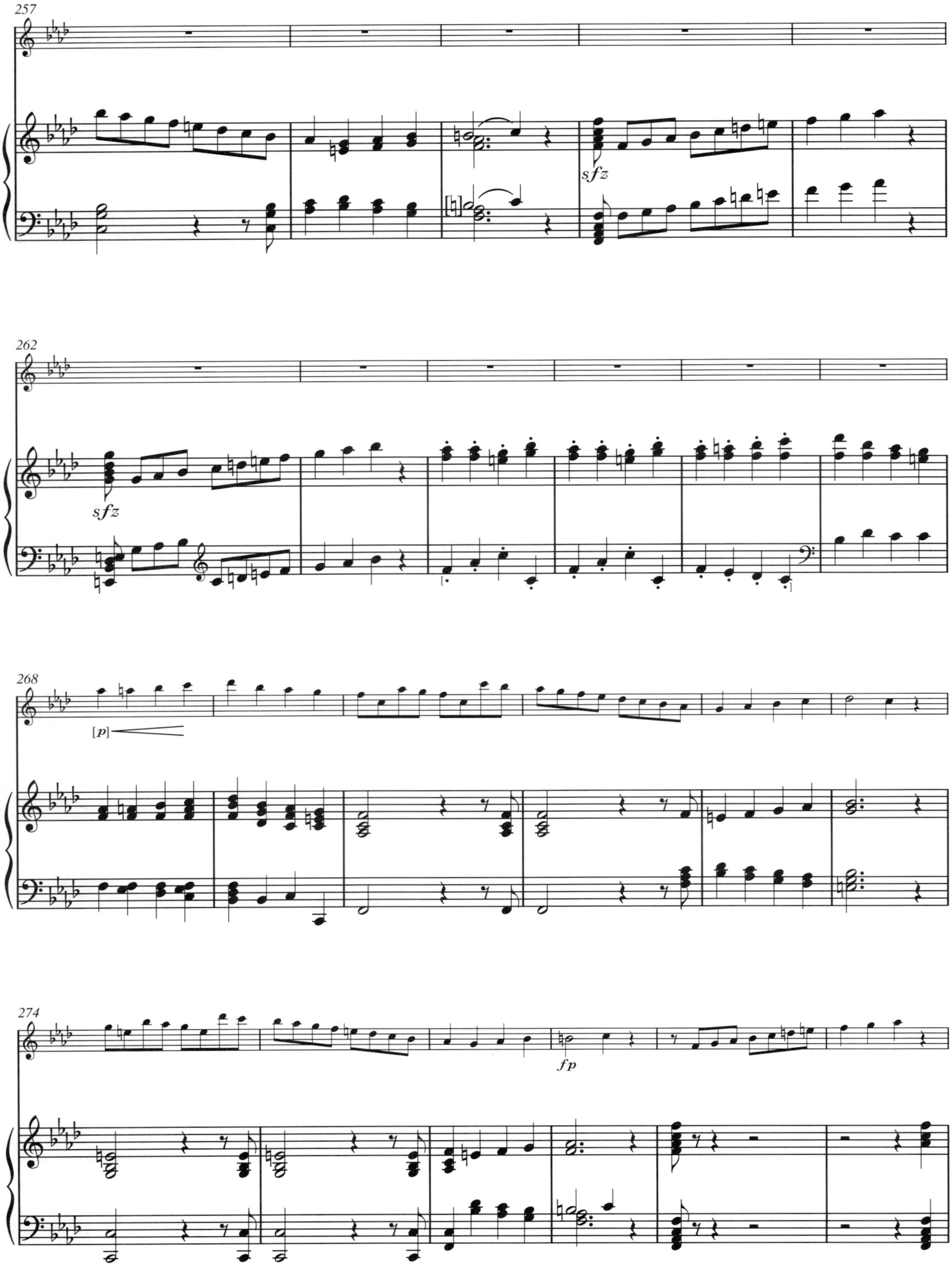

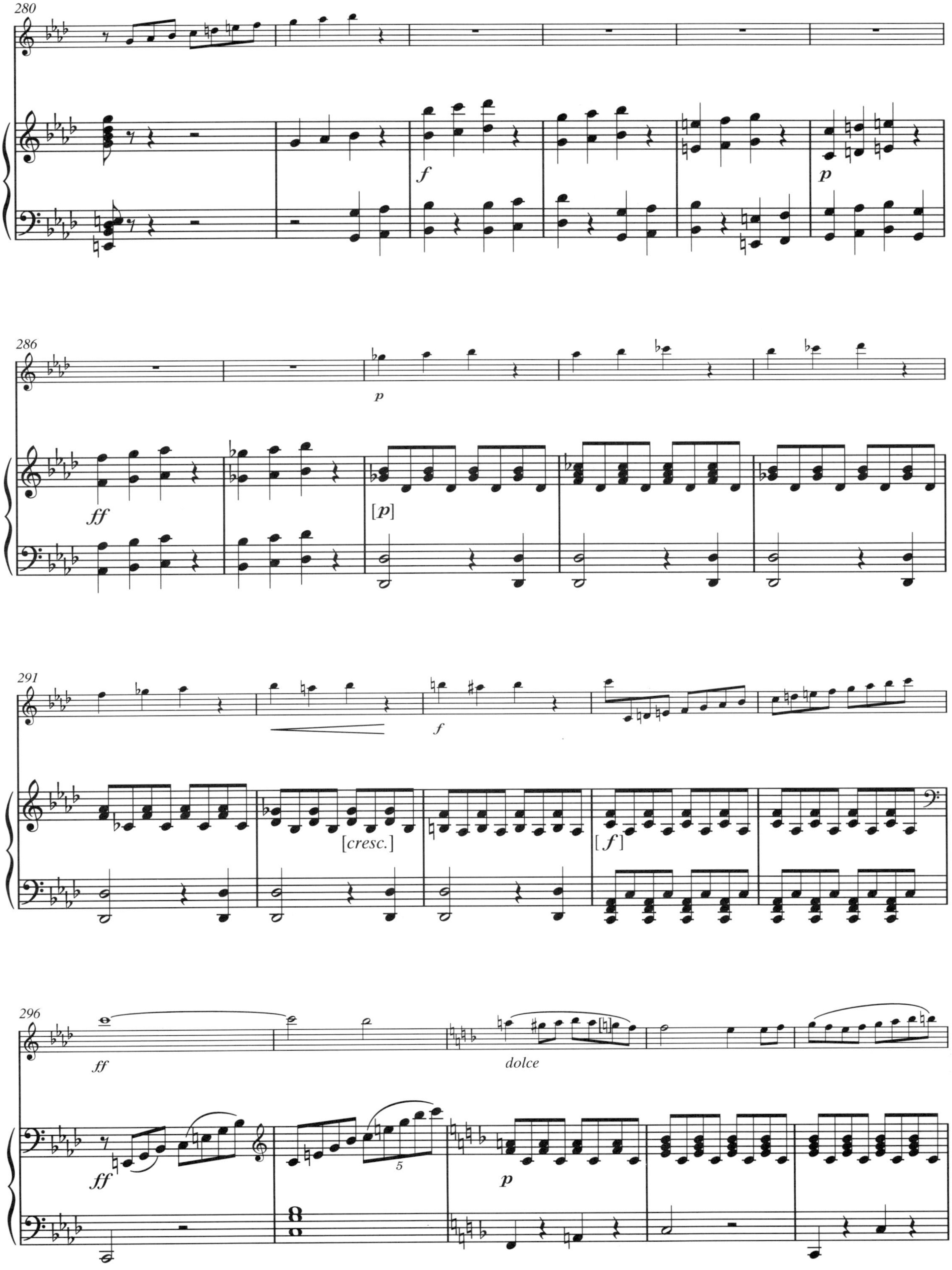
280
286
291
[cresc.]
296
dolce

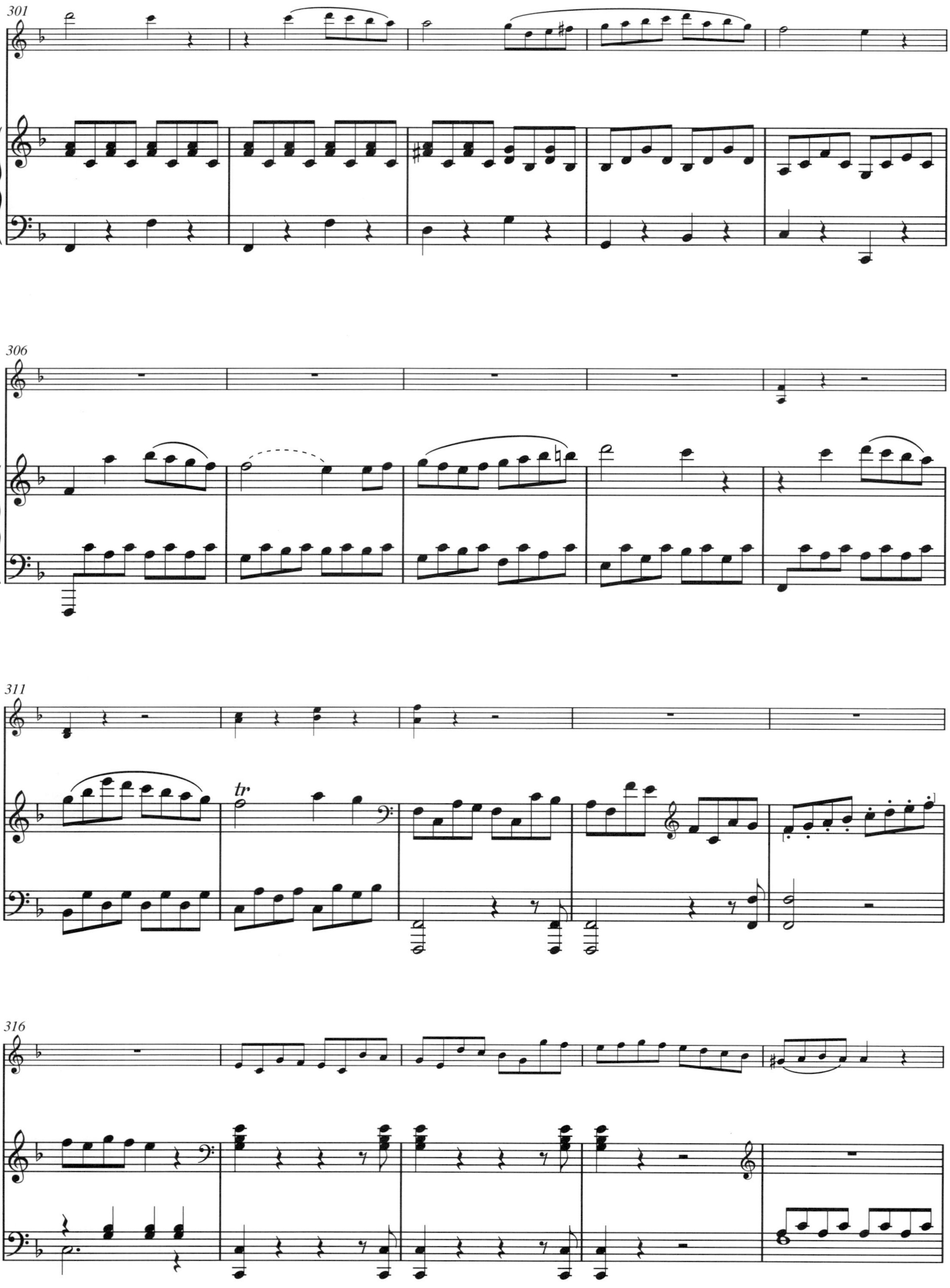
301
306
311
tr
316

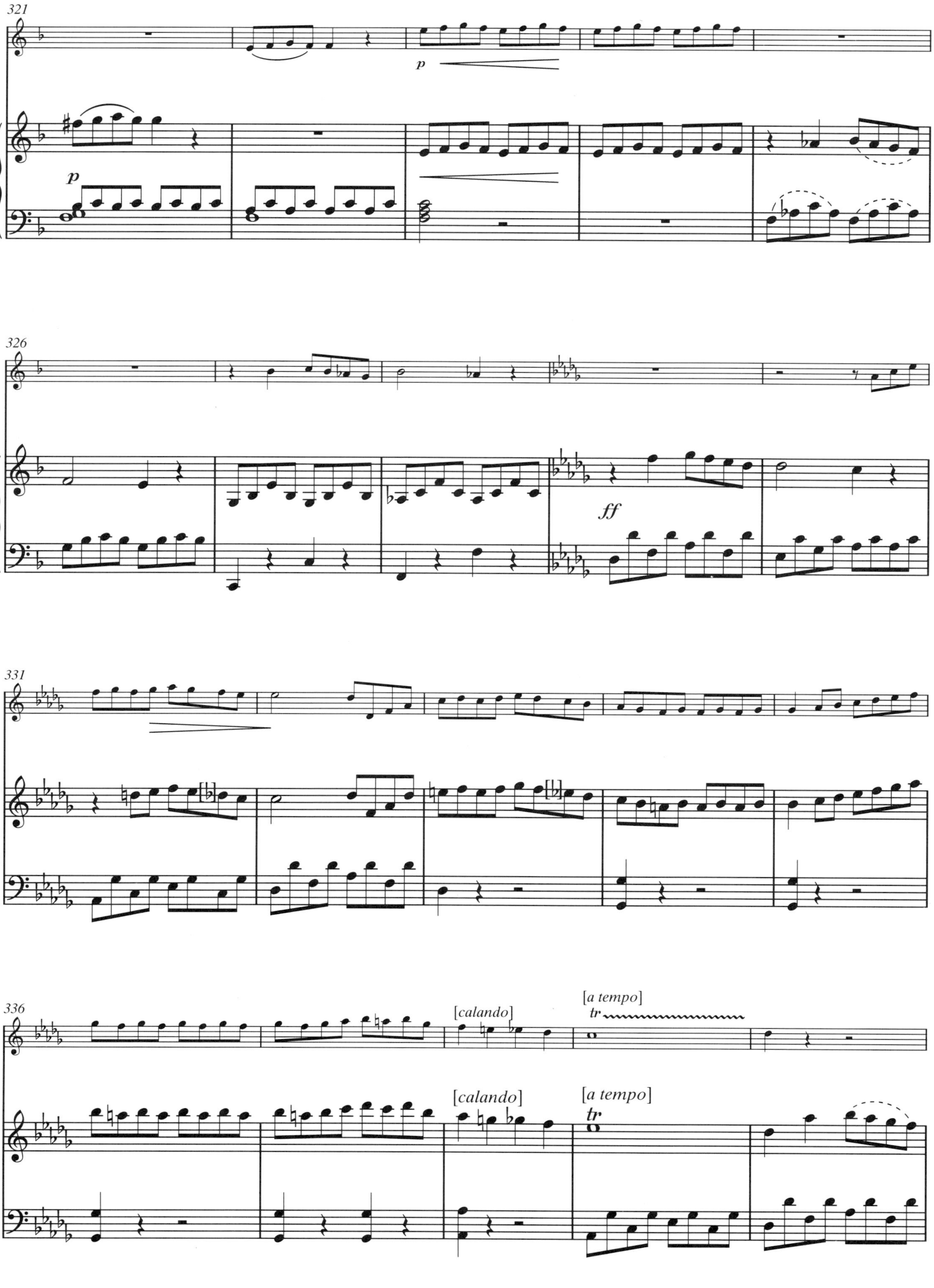
321
p
p
326
ff
331
336
[calando]
[a tempo]
tr
[calando]
[a tempo]
tr

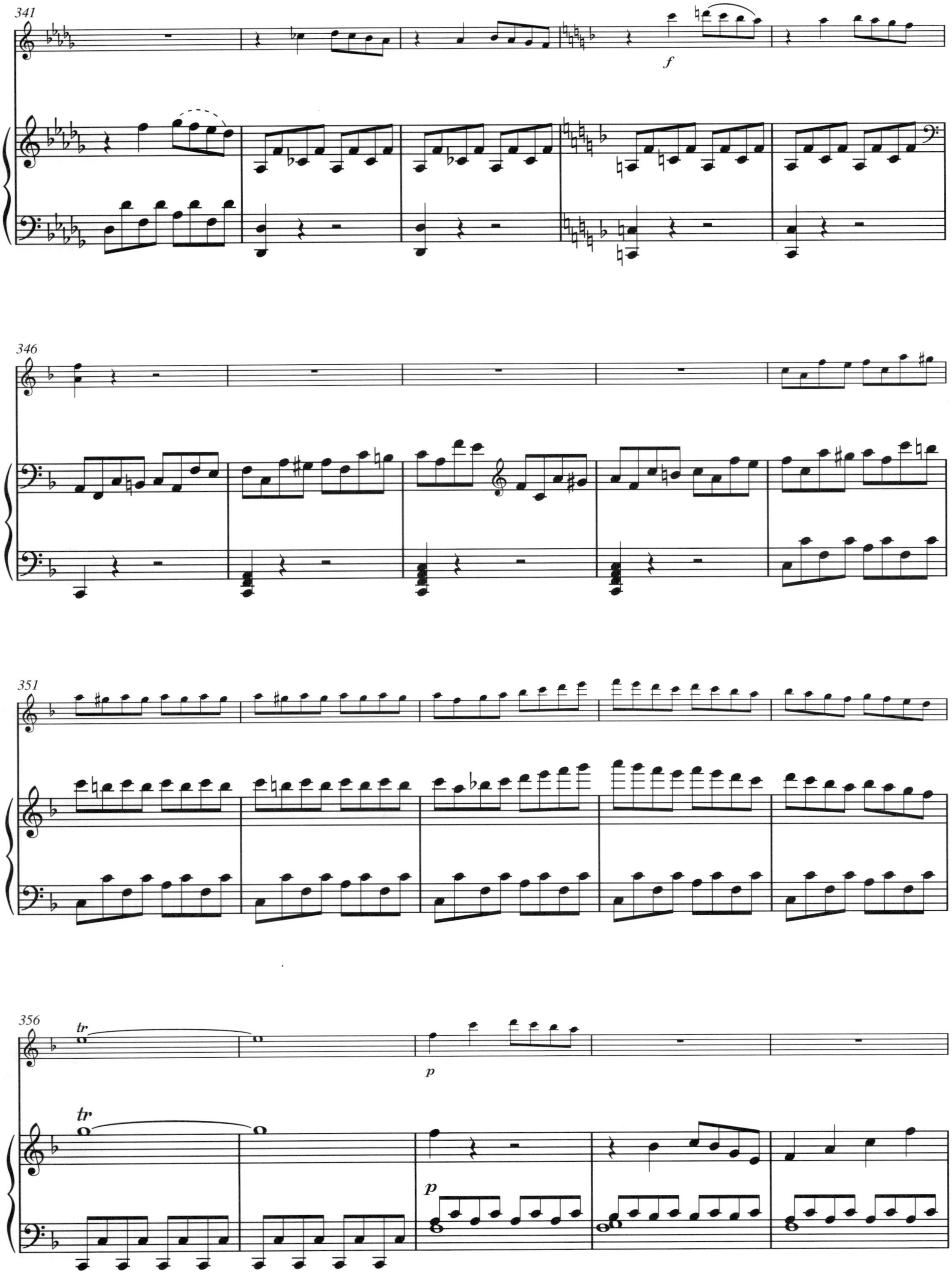
341
f
346
351
356
tr
tr
p
p

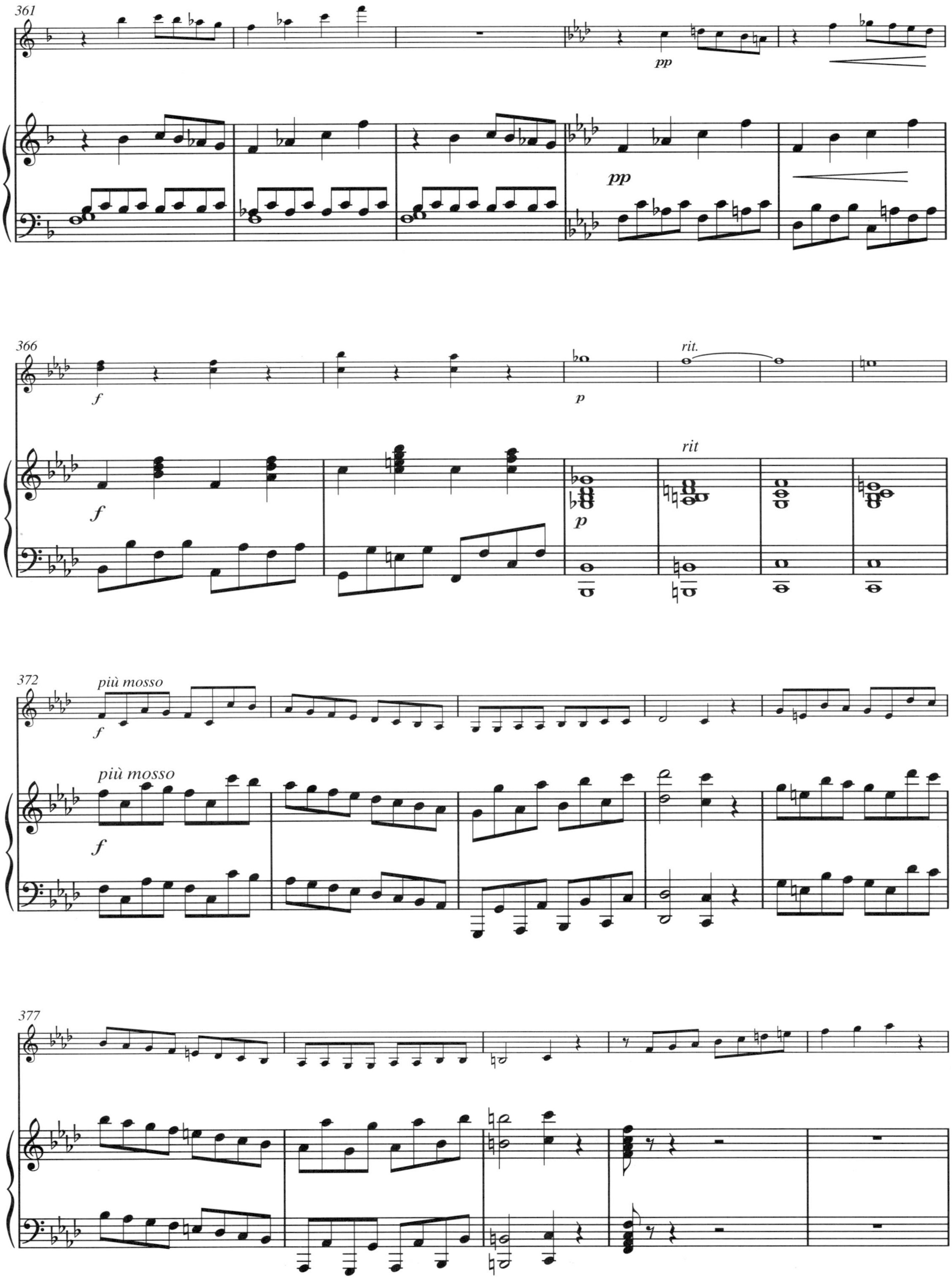
361
pp
pp
366
f
f
p
rit.
rit
p
372
più mosso
f
più mosso
f
377

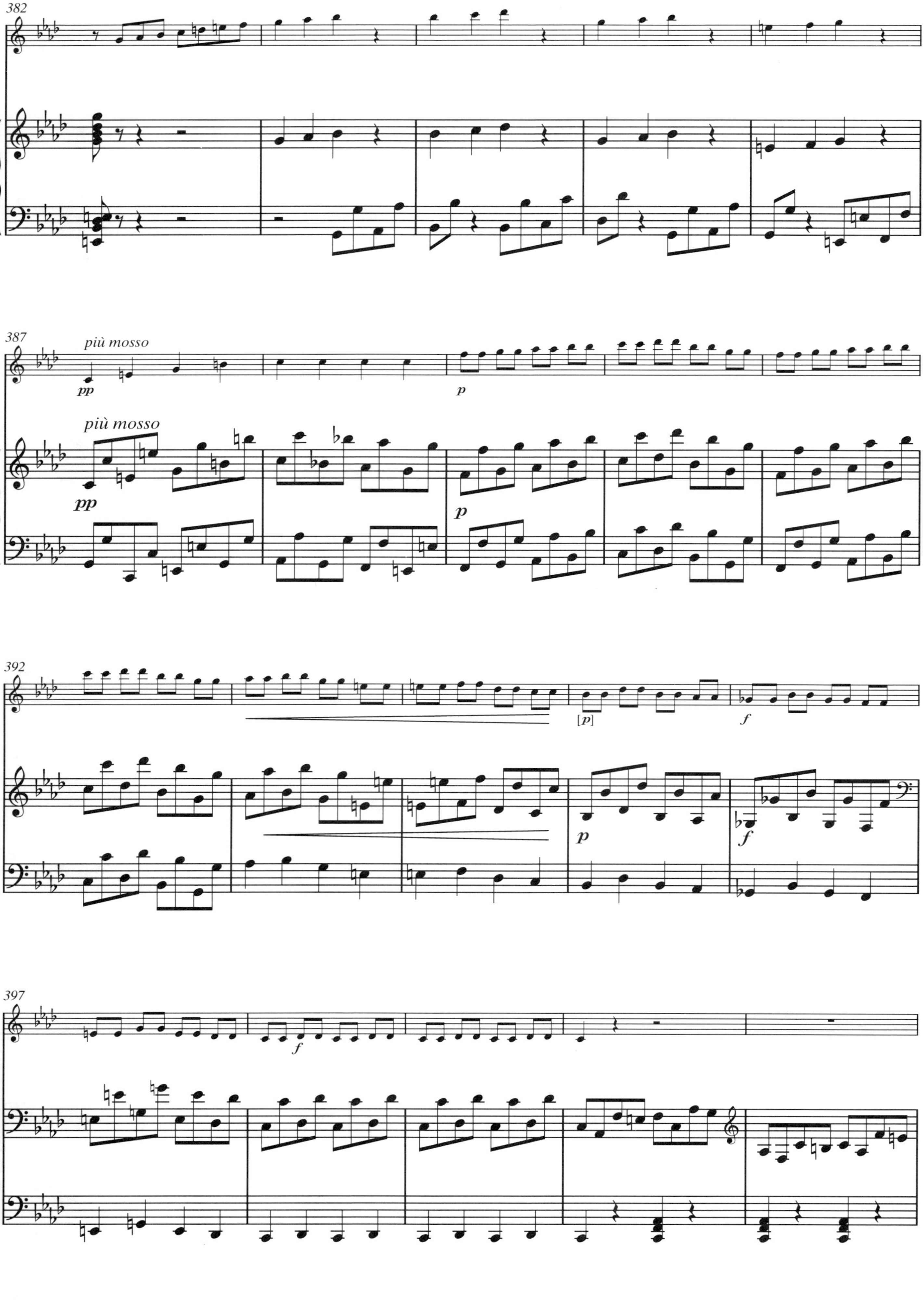
382
387
più mosso
pp
più mosso
pp
p
p
392
[p]
f
p
f
397
f

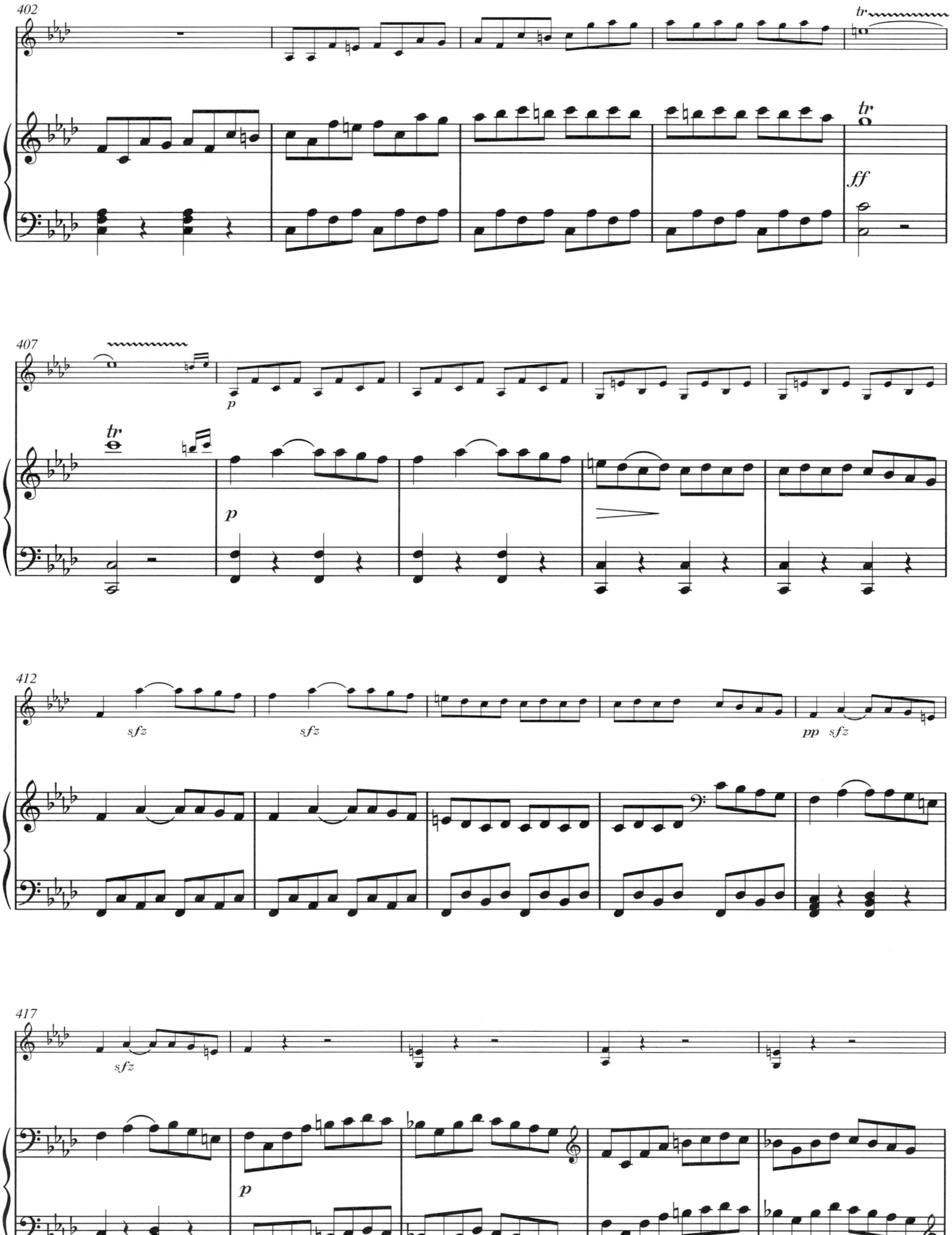
402
tr
tr
ff
407
tr
p
p
412
sfz
sfz
pp sfz
417
sfz
p

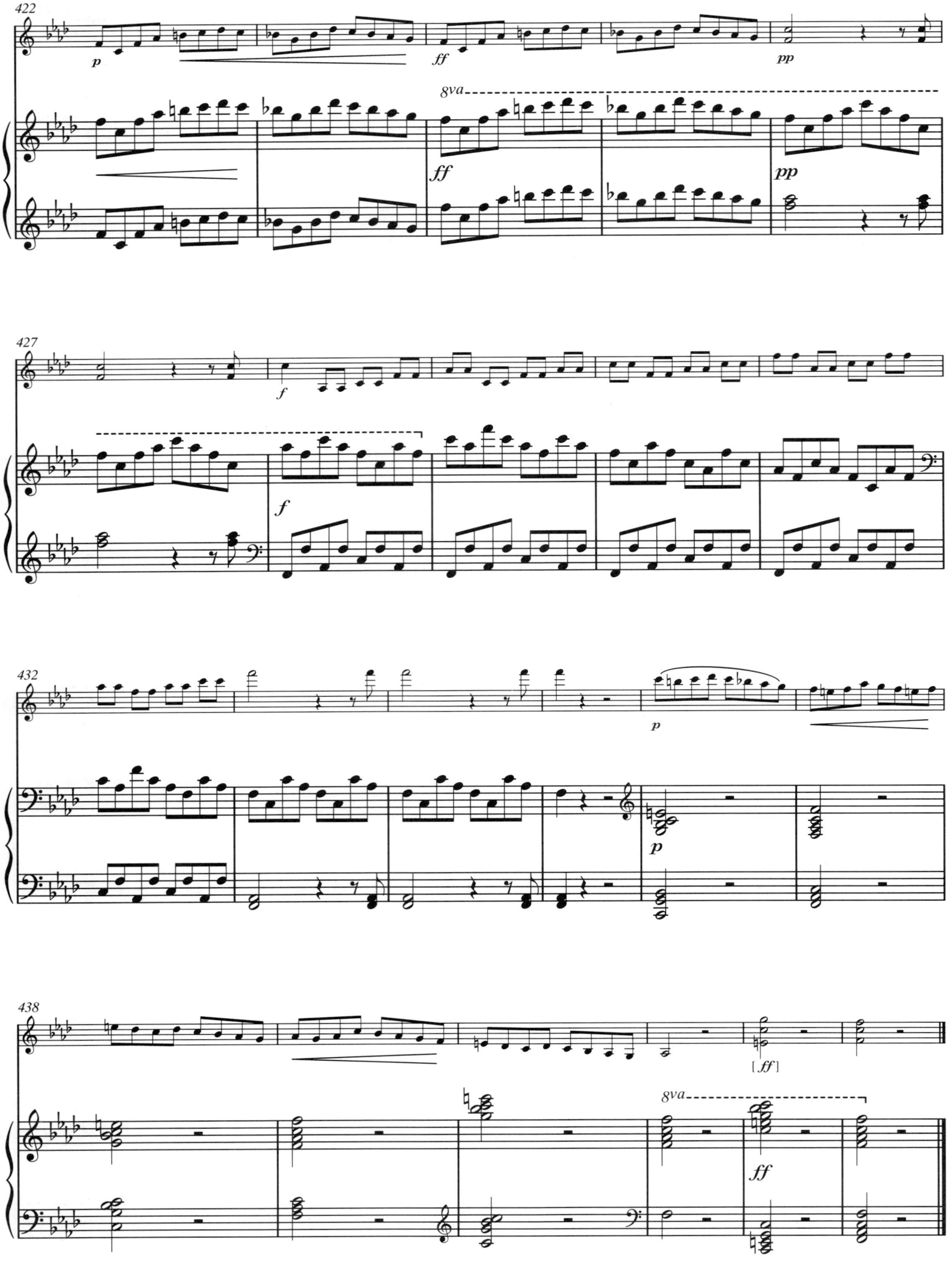
422
p
ff
pp
8va
ff
pp
427
f
f
432
p
p
438
[ff]
8va
ff

APPENDIX 1

Beethoven's Emendations to the *Forty Variations*
Facsimile and Transcription of CS-KRa A 4375

CS-KRa A 4375, [page 1], unpaginated

KEY

Staff
Staves   *Location*

1–2   [1] var. 36, m. 247; [2] var. 38, m. 358; [3] var. 39, m. 413

3–4   [4] var. 40, mm. 455–56; [5] var. 40, m. 469

5–6   [6] var. 40, m. 472; [7] var. 40, m. 500; [8] var. 40, m. 535

7–8   [9] var. 40, m. 536; [10] var. 40, mm. 609–10; [11] var. 40, mm. 649–50

9–10   [12] var. 40, m. 690

11–12   [13] not identified; [14] var. 35, m. 232; [15] not identified; [16] var. 29, m. 209; [17] var. 40, mm. 521–22

CS-KRa A 4375, [page 2], unpaginated

KEY

Staff/Staves	Location
1–2	[A] pencil sketch in Rudolph's hand (cf. intro., mm. 21–22, mm. 69–74)
3–4	[B] pencil sketch in Rudolph's hand; [18] var. 40, m. 742; [19] var. 9, m. 128
5	[20] intro., m. 3; [21] intro., m. 45
6–7	[22] var. 40, mm. 645–47
9–10	[23] intro., m. 3; [24] intro., m. 20; [25] intro., m. 47; [26] intro., m. 58; [27] intro., m. 71
11–12	[28] var. 7, m. 119; [29] var. 9, m. 128; [30] var. 21, m. 178; [31] var. 23, m. 183; [32] var. 12, m. 137; [33] var. 12, m. 138; [34] var. 12, m. 139

CS-KRa A 4375, [page 3], paginated "2" in pencil

109

KEY

Staff/
Staves   *Location*

1–2   [35] ("No. 1") var. 10, m. 132; [36] ("No. 2") var. 11, m. 135

4–5   [36] ("No. 2"), cntd.; [37] ("No. 3") var. 13, m. 143

7–9   [38] ("No. 4") var. 27, m. 200; [39] ("No. 5") var. 29, mm. 207–8

10–11   [39] ("No. 5"), cntd. (m. 208); [40] ("No. 6") var. 39, mm. 392–93

CS-KRa A 4375, [page 4], unpaginated

KEY

Staff/Staves	Location
1–2	[41] ("No. 7") var. 40, fugue, mm. 693–94
4–5	[42] ("No. 8") var. 40, fugue, m. 706; [43] ("No. 9") var. 40, fugue, mm. 708–9
7–8	[41] ("No. 9"), cntd. (m. 709)
10–11	[44] ("No. 10") var. 40, fugue, m. 741

CS-KRa A 4375, [page 5], paginated "2" in ink

KEY

Staff/
Staves   *Location*

1–2   [45] ("No. 11") var. 40, fugue, m. 747; [46] ("No. 12") var. 40, fugue, m. 753

APPENDIX 2

Sonata in F Minor for Violin and Piano
Earlier Version
Facsimiles of CS-KRa A 4405, A 4407

CS-KRa A 4405, unpaginated, Allegro, [page 1] (above) and [page 2] (below)

CS-KRa A 4405, unpaginated, Allegro, [page 3] (above) and [page 4] (below)

CS-KRa A 4405, unpaginated, Allegro, [page 5] (above) and [page 6] (below)

CS-KRa A 4405, unpaginated, Allegro, [page 7] (above) and [page 8] (below)

CS-KRa A 4405, unpaginated, Allegro, [page 9] (above) and [page 10] (below)

CS-KRa A 4405, unpaginated, Allegro, [page 11] (above) and [page 12] (below)

CS-KRa A 4405, unpaginated, Allegro, [page 13] (above) and [page 14] (below)

CS-KRa A 4405, unpaginated, Scherzo. Allegro, [page 1] (above) and [page 2] (below)

CS-KRa A 4405, unpaginated, Finale. Allegro assai, [page 1] (above) and [page 2] (below)

CS-KRa A 4405, unpaginated, Finale. Allegro assai, [page 3] (above) and [page 4] (below)

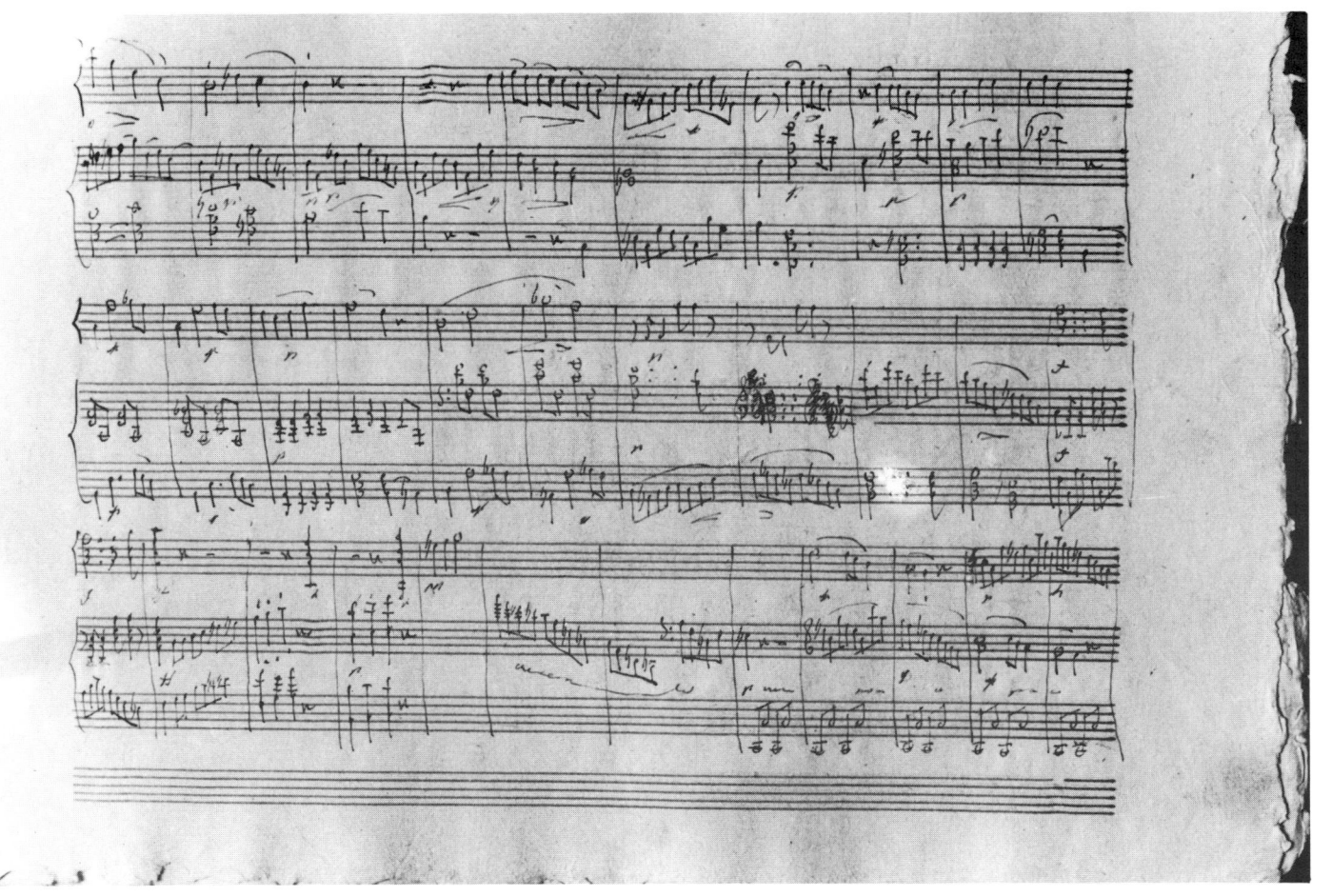

CS-KRa A 4405, unpaginated, Finale. Allegro assai, [page 5] (above) and [page 6] (below)

CS-KRa A 4405, unpaginated, Finale. Allegro assai, [page 7] (above) and [page 8] (below)

CS-KRa A 4405, unpaginated, Finale. Allegro assai, [page 9] (above) and [page 10] (below)

CS-KRa A 4405, unpaginated, Finale. Allegro assai, [page 11] (above) and [page 12] (below)

CS-KRa A 4405, unpaginated, Finale. Allegro assai, [page 13] (above) and [page 14] (below)

CS-KRa A 4407, unpaginated, Adagio con esspressione, [page 1] (above) and [page 2] (below)

CS-KRa A 4407, unpaginated, Adagio con esspressione, [page 3] (above) and [page 4] (below)

CS-KRa A 4407, unpaginated, Adagio con esspressione, [page 5]

CS-KRa A 4407, unpaginated, [Adagio] draft, [page 1] (above) and [page 2] (below)

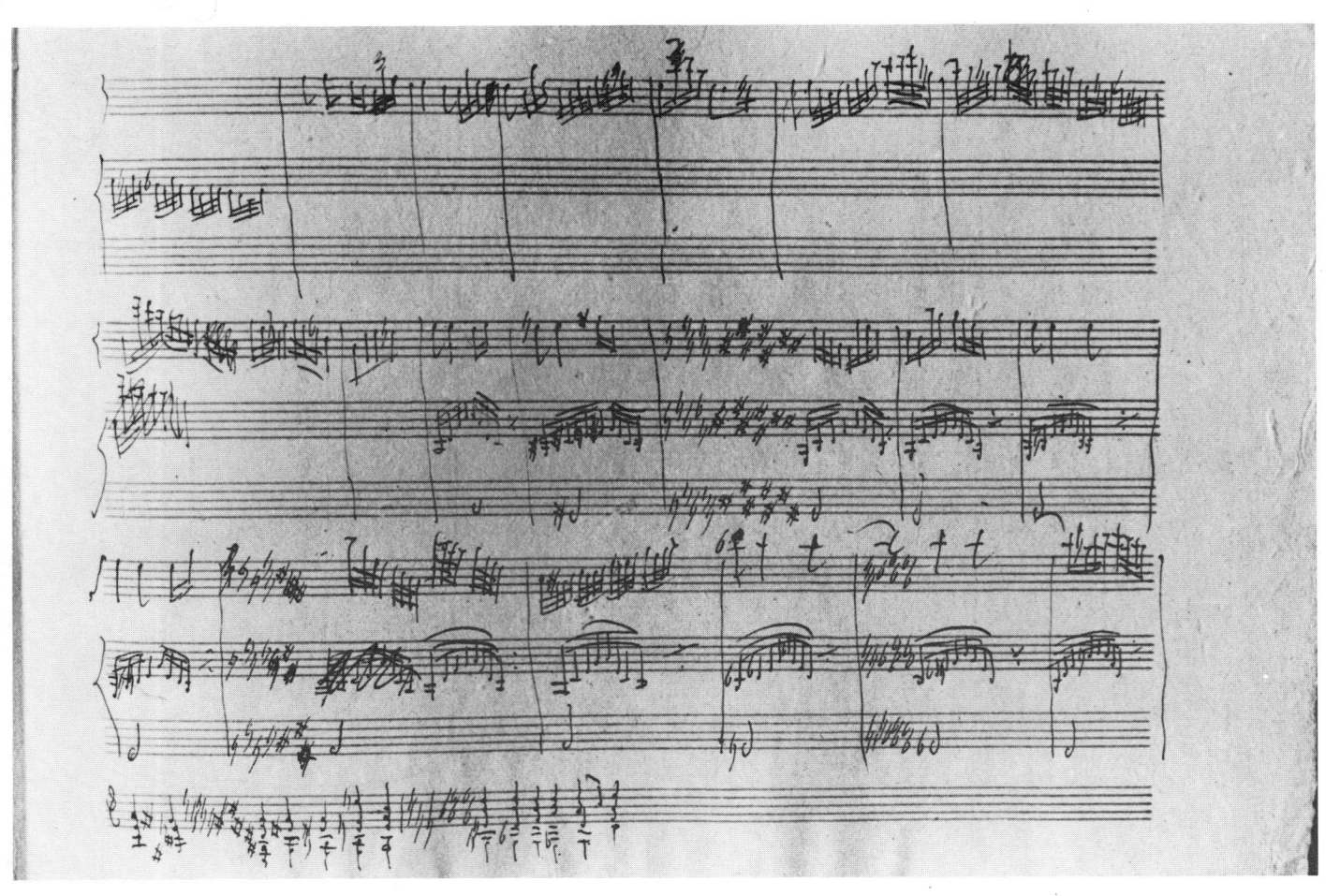

CS-KRa A 4407, unpaginated, [Adagio] draft, [page 3] (above) and [page 4] (below)

M2.R23834 v.21 Q
  Rudolph, Archduke of Austria,
  1788-1831.
    Forty variations on a theme by
Beethoven.

DATE DUE

M2.R23834 v.21 Q
  Rudolph, Archduke of Austria,
  1788-1831.
    Forty variations on a theme by
Beethoven.